Homework for Learning
300 Practical Strategies

WE...

...her t(

Homework for Learning
300 Practical Strategies

Gerry Czerniawski and Warren Kidd

 Open University Press

Open University Press
McGraw-Hill Education
McGraw-Hill House
Shoppenhangers Road
Maidenhead
Berkshire
England
SL6 2QL

email: enquiries@openup.co.uk
world wide web: www.openup.co.uk

and Two Penn Plaza, New York, NY 10121-2289, USA

First published 2013

A catalogue record of this book is available from the British Library

ISBN-13: 978-0-33-524589-5 (pb)
ISBN-10: 0-335-24589-7 (pb)
eISBN: 978-0-33-524590-1

Library of Congress Cataloging-in-Publication Data
CIP data applied for

Typeset by Aptara, Inc.

Fictitious names of companies, products, people, characters and/or data that may be used herein (in case studies or in examples) are not intended to represent any real individual, company, product or event.

Praise for this book

"*Homework for Learning* is an important read for both new and experienced teachers looking for inspiration. Written in an engaging and highly accessible manner the authors offer a persuasive and powerful argument as to why teachers need to consider the transformative potential of learning outside of the classroom. The practical strategies offered are underpinned by grounded evidence and a research base which encourages us to rethink our homework practices. The emphasis upon 'looking back and looking forwards', supported by critical reflective practice, action research and ongoing professional development is timely. This will be a 'must read' text in my institution."

Julie Hughes, Head of Department (Post Compulsory Education),
University of Wolverhampton, UK

"Within the first few pages Gerry and Warren's book captured my interest. Firstly they openly talk about the problems around homework, something I could fully empathise with. Then they discuss how homework can be used more creatively to support independent learning and learning that involves others in the process. This is not only a very practical book with extensive guidance on good practice for teachers, it also draws on literature that challenges some of our pre-conceptions about what homework should 'look like'. Through a series of activity sheets, suggestions, thinking points and professional development ideas, the authors challenge teachers to think more carefully about the reasons for setting homework, what they are trying to achieve from it and how they might best support students. What is more, this book is stuffed full of fun ideas for homework that represent innovative approaches likely to engage the interest of students and move beyond the traditional essay (although this is also included). Not only will these suggestions improve the experiences of students, it will also be much more fun for teachers in giving and utilising the homework set."

Dr Linda Hammersley-Fletcher, Manchester Metropolitan University, UK

"This is a really useful book. Written in a clear style, Gerry Czerniawski and Warren Kidd draw on a wealth of classroom experience and research to share some powerful ideas about learning and teaching. For this book is not just about homework but about how to teach so that children learn. It has heaps of tips and strategies underpinned by big educational ideas that will really excite all sorts of teachers, not just those new to the profession, and get pupils engaged. Inspirational!"

Dr Sara Bubb, Institute of Education, UK

Gerry dedicates this book to Jenny Barksfield for her endless love and patience during the writing process.

Warren would like to dedicate this book to his partner Jane and his son Freddie. Thank you for your continued support.

Contents

List of tables and figures

Tables

Figures

Acknowledgments

Both authors would like to acknowledge the continued help and support of Jean Murray and Ann Slater at the Cass School of Education and Communities University of East London. We would also like to thank the following people for their advice and guidance with some of the ideas: Vikki Barrowcliff, Vanessa Fantie, Phil Robinson, Kate Jones, Elicia Lewis, Chris Dalladay, Erica Cattle, Sarah Meredith, David Wells, Gordon Davis, Nadim Dimechkie, Richard Sparham, Jeanette Waller, Mark Ivory and Sarah Roberts.

Finally we thank Richard Woff at the British Museum for his inspirational ideas on the use of museums in teaching and learning.

Introduction: how to use this book

Drawing upon our experience as teachers and now as teacher educators we really value the learning opportunities that homework has provided our learners. *Homework for Learning* is essential. We see clearly that homework (and learning outside the classroom in a wider sense) has fundamentally contributed to learner motivation, outstanding examination achievement and an extremely positive relationship with those we have taught. It enables a productive classroom atmosphere and culture. And yet, this is but one side of the story. We are very conscious that homework seems increasingly to occupy a contradictory place in today's schools and colleges. On the one hand, some teachers feel homework has little value or they recognize the difficulties in getting some learners to take homework seriously. On the other, teachers also feel that curriculum time, with each successive government reform, is becoming even further 'squeezed' – perhaps positioning homework as more important and the lack of attention given to homework even more problematic. Equally, if we believe the media, homework (and in particular, coursework) is increasingly seen as a burden not only for learners but also for teachers and parents, both of whom might overly support some learners with their work. Alongside these issues we also see in many countries growing concerns over teachers' workload, assessment burdens, and bureaucratic logging and tracking systems in schools and colleges. What makes the picture interesting is that alongside all this, since the early 2000s the teaching profession has almost completely re-thought its relationship to assessment, marking and feedback. However homework has been left behind, and in some cases almost completely forgotten. In other cases, in different places and institutions, homework flourishes as do homework and assessment cultures. So, why the difference? And what can we do to develop homework cultures and practices of our own?

As experienced practitioners and teacher educators our view on and relationship to homework are different to the picture we paint above. We have extensive experience of working with non-traditional learners in urban settings and in partnership with these learners, their parents and our colleagues obtaining the highest measurements of success possible. Homework, for us, has always played a key role in this success and with the appropriate learning environment, expectations and ethos homework has never been 'problematic'. Far from it, in fact. We have seen through our own practice that all learners of all abilities can successfully complete and value homework, as long as its relationship to the learner, the curriculum and to classroom strategies is well defined. In this book, we refer to this approach as a '*Homework for Learning*' (HfL) approach.

Get creative with homework strategies!

Creativity, energy and openness are the hallmarks of a great teacher and it is this spirit that engulfs the ethos behind this book. We take an unusual approach to homework arguing that far from being a finishing-off activity or separate learning strategy, all 'homework' should be inextricably related and complementary to the teaching and learning that take place *in* the classroom. In particular we believe that 'homework' is not something that should necessarily be done at home. When imaginatively and considerately deployed, homework can be carried out anywhere; can promote independent learning; can assist in the development of generic skills; and can free up time for further work on any curriculum. The suggestions for homework strategies in this text will be underpinned by a range of educational theories on learning as well as expert practice that both authors have witnessed in many of the schools and colleges they regularly visit.

In this book we argue that homework is not just a strategy for raising achievement. It can instil passion, motivation and enthusiasm for the subject in the hearts and minds of *all* learners irrespective of ability. Properly structured and facilitated homework can add one year to a student's full time education (Stern 2009). It can promote individual pride and success in learners and can often generate the most creative and memorable work a student ever does (e.g. that project; that podcast; that painting; that prize winning essay). Finally, homework provides all teachers with invaluable evidence of learner engagement with their subject and their teaching strategies. As such it is an invaluable source of summative, formative and ipsative assessment of teaching and learning. In this book we therefore include suggestions that offer a variety of assessment opportunities but above all ensure that these practical and accessible ideas motivate and energize learners to learn further. Thus, homework is *for* learning (HfL), and is a considerable factor in extending learning further.

Key principles

This book is based upon the following six principles:

1. It offers practical ideas on the use of homework – for experienced and non-experienced colleagues alike.
2. It provides support for trainee teachers on homework to improve grade and lesson observation profiles by focusing on the role that homework can play in raising achievement.
3. In discussing homework and learning outside the classroom, the book explores the theoretical and academic underpinnings of these issues which student teachers and in-service professional learners (be they taking Initial Teacher Education qualifications or Masters level accreditation) need to pass written assignments.

4. The spirit of the book is that all educational professionals need both a theoretical and practical recognition of the important role homework and 'outside of the class' learning have to play in informing personalization, differentiation and lesson planning.
5. The book offers strategies for marking and assessing homework and for the logging and recording of this data.
6. Finally, we seek to incorporate issues of e-Learning (electronic learning) and M-learning (mobile learning) into homework practice.

A note about terms

We have said this is a book about 'homework' and yet, increasingly, this is a book about learning 'outside of the classroom' in the wider sense. We mean by this that 'homework' might increasingly be a misnomer. It might be the case that learning outside of the class happens in informal IT suites (maybe linked to library services) or in school and college canteens with Wi-Fi access. Learning might be 'on the move' through digital portable devices or on buses or trains as part of a journey to and from school and college. For older learners, with a degree of unstructured private study time and examination study leave, learning outside of the class might still take place on the premises of the institution, but be structured less formally.

How to use this book

Our view is that both new and experienced teachers are always looking for new ideas – especially ideas that might be 'easy' or require little preparation. While acknowledging current theoretical debates the spirit of this book is 'this is what works'; the book offers practical ideas covering:

- developing research skills
- motivation and learning
- homework as a starter activity
- strategies to ensure high homework completion rates
- ideas for exam preparation
- using technology, E-learning and M-learning strategies
- coursework and project preparation
- strategies for personalized learning
- supporting Gifted and Talented cohorts
- marking and assessment strategies
- assessment for learning
- differentiation
- thinking skills

Chapter outline

The book is divided into three parts:

- **Part 1** of the book is designed to equip teachers with the variety of theories, debates, concepts and best practice associated with homework as an assessment practice.
- **Part 2** consists of one single chapter comprised of 300 numbered strategies for homework divided into themes that are associated with the ideas examined in Part 1.
- **Part 3** is comprised of the final concluding chapter. We seek to position homework as a nexus of teacher reflection, continuing professional development and action research. This concluding chapter suggests ways that teachers can generate their own ideas for out-of-classroom strategies based around the voices and needs of their own learners.

In Chapter 7 (Part 2) we provide 300 ideas for homework and learning outside of the classroom. To make these accessible we have collated the ideas and strategies under the following headings:

- **See it!**
- **Read it!**
- **Hear it!**
- **Move it!**
- **Think it!**
- **Chat it!**
- **Revise it!**
- **Research it!**
- **E-it!**
- **M-it!**

In Chapter 7 we try and link homework ideas to starter activities in the text itself to help you with your planning and preparation. Where you see this icon 🏃 you know that the strategy under discussion would be excellent to try to incorporate into a starter activity.

Throughout part one of the book we will signpost both short ideas for *'best practice'* and also those essential *'links between theory and practice'*. We will also draw upon our experience in offering advice and *'frequently asked questions'*. You will come across these boxes from time to time in the text, and collectively they should help you to reflect upon the issues under discussion and link them to your own practice in a more concrete way. We finish each chapter with *'questions for professional development'* for you to continue this reflective practice further.

We hope that through using this book we can encourage you to experiment with our strategies, adapting them to your own practice.

Part 1

What do you need to know? Laying the foundations for best practice

1 Homework for learning

Chapter objectives

In this chapter we will:

- examine the arguments for and against homework;
- introduce the educational theories underpinning the homework strategies in this book;
- explore the implications from research informed practice on the successful implementation of all homework strategies;
- discuss factors that need to be embedded in successful institutional homework policies.

Introduction – it's all in the name

When was the last time you heard anyone talk enthusiastically about 'homework'? For many, the very word embodies a labyrinth of emotions encompassing boredom, conflict, compulsion, trepidation and punishment. Many teachers contribute to this narrative by setting homework as a finishing-off activity just before the bell goes or by threatening to 'set homework' if their Year 9s don't or won't 'behave'. Henderson (2006: 23) makes the rather sad point that 'whilst learning in school [has] apparently become more varied, more differentiated and more imaginative, learning outside of the school [seems] to be stuck in a time warp where the tasks lack a quality of thinking as to the needs of the learner'. In this book we believe that all homework, regardless of the type of institution or target age group, should be '*Homework for Learning*' (HfL) i.e. an essential tool for Assessment for Learning (AfL). Homework tasks that are imaginatively conceived, enthusiastically facilitated and creatively deployed can stimulate curiosity, innovation and a passion for any subject. When successfully implemented homework strategies can become the bedrock for stretching and challenging all learners, regardless of their ability. Even more than this, HfL can provide invaluable opportunities to assess the progress of learners and enable all teachers to critically reflect on the extent to which their teaching strategies are successful.

Conceived differently by those it affects, the multifaceted nature of homework can involve complex interactions between and within two contexts – the institution in which the tasks are generated and the home of the learner for whom the task has been created. Cooper's (1989) classic definition describes homework as 'tasks assigned to students by school [sic] teachers that are meant to be carried out during non-school hours' (Cooper 1989: 7) and while this definition may be fit for purpose in a number of scenarios it cannot satisfy the scope and remit of the book you are about to read. In the following chapters we examine the roles that homework and 'outside of the class learning' play in teaching and learning and curriculum construction. This text speaks directly to the professional learner offering advice and strategies for setting, marking and using homework to inform personalization, AfL and lesson planning in all sorts of learning institutions and for all sorts of learners.

We argue that far from being a finishing-off activity or separate learning strategy, all homework should be inextricably related and complementary to, the teaching and learning that takes place *in* the classroom, studio or workshop. Homework for Learning (HfL) provides opportunities to invest time outside of lessons in developing learners' thinking skills and essential research skills to enable school and college learners of today to become lifelong learners of tomorrow.

A Pandora's Box for researchers

For educational researchers, getting to grips with the extent to which homework supports or impedes learning has proven a hard nut to crack. When talking about educational achievement, it is, for example, very difficult to separate homework as a factor from other variables including the quality of teaching, resources, parental support and so on. The time people spend on homework can also vary enormously depending on who you talk to and for what reasons. Learners, their parents/guardians and teachers may have very good reasons for exaggerating, for example, the time spent on doing, supporting, preparing and marking homework depending on whether the person they are talking to is a friend, partner, parent, teacher or line manager. Methodologically speaking different research studies on homework have deployed different research methods (e.g. surveys, interviews, observation) making comparison of the effects of homework on learners problematic. Nevertheless a number of points emerge from the research (Hallam 2005; Hancock 2001) that should be born in mind when setting homework:

- In general high ability students get set more homework than the less able.
- Learners say that teacher expectation is one of the most decisive factors in motivating them to complete homework tasks.
- Learners like homework to be directly linked to the lesson.

- Teachers say that the most important function of homework is reinforcement, review and practice of content.

Much of the published research on homework has tended to focus more on subjects that prioritize their quantitative dimensions (e.g. mathematics and science) and less on those subjects where the quality of writing and expression of ideas (e.g. history and English) are central to the discipline, adding to the difficulties researchers face. With comparatively little research available on the effects of homework on the post-16 environment it is also difficult to assess the impact that homework has on vocational subjects (e.g. business studies, hairdressing, and design and technology). Finally most research on homework has tended to explore the effects homework has on achievement often ignoring the impact that learning outside the classroom can have on motivation and a lifelong interest in the subject.

Why do we set 'homework'?

Accepting the fact that homework is a hard nut to crack for researchers on educational achievement makes it easier to accept that there are arguments both for and against homework as a strategy for raising achievement coming from leading experts in the field (e.g. Cooper 1989; Hallam 2005; Kohn 2006; Patell et al. 2009). These arguments are summarized below:

Arguments for:

1. Homework increases knowledge and understanding of the subject, factual retention, critical reasoning and curriculum enrichment.
2. It nurtures the independent learner (e.g. fostering self-direction, self-discipline, time management, inquisitiveness, creativity and research skills).
3. It is beneficial for schools/colleges by easing time constraints on the curriculum, exploiting resources not available in the institution thus fulfilling the expectations of parents, learners, politicians and the public.
4. Homework can involve parents/guardians/schools/colleges in a potentially dynamic and supportive set of relationships that result in greater participation and academic achievement.

Arguments against:

1. It can create physical and emotional fatigue and a loss of interest in the subject.
2. While homework can involve greater participation between parents, learners and their institutions of learning it can also become a site of conflict between each of these stakeholders.

3. Homework can interfere with other extra-curricular activities, hobbies and part-time employment opportunities.
4. Left unmonitored, homework activities can foster cheating and strategic surface-level engagement with the subject.

All of the arguments above are worth taking seriously, however in this book we argue that raising learner achievement in the short term is but one of many reasons why outstanding teachers succeed in inspiring and nurturing their learners. We also accept the arguments against homework when homework strategies are poorly designed, implemented and assessed. Our homework strategies are designed to be used by all teachers to ignite curiosity and a desire to learn beyond the immediate and very understandable concerns of exams, coursework deadlines, college entry requirements and employability. Outstanding teachers succeed in fostering a long-term love and critical engagement in their disciplines, in part, by their ability to motivate and foster curiosity, critical engagement and a passion for learning. It is therefore worth remembering two points when setting homework:

1. The effects of homework on academic achievement increase the older the learner is.
2. Any negative effects of homework and its inability as a strategy to raise achievement are often the result of the misuse of homework as a teaching strategy and poor communication on the part of many teachers.

Not *another* essay! Educational theory and homework

The strategies in this book have been strongly influenced by a range of educational theories but it is important to realize that theories are just that – theories! They are the products of the particular historical and social context in which they are generated, importing ideas from other disciplines such as psychology, sociology and biology. In many cases they are also informed by political agendas and scientific, technological and popularist thinking and it is therefore important that teachers constantly update their understanding of these theories while keeping an open and critical mind to new ideas informing the profession, for example, the significant impact in recent years that neuroscience is having on everything we have learnt about teaching and learning including homework.

Malcolm Knowles (1980) makes a clear philosophical distinction between the use of the terms 'pedagogy' and 'andragogy' when referring to the characteristics and values of teachers and learners. Pedagogy (originally referring to the teaching of children) implies a dependency on the teacher by the learner. The teacher is cast as a figure of authority who assumes that readiness to learn is uniform by age and curriculum. Knowles argues that this is in stark contrast to andragogy (referring to the teaching of adults). This distinction casts the learner in a far more self-directed and autonomous role. The teacher is viewed as a guide and facilitator in which the readiness to learn is not uniform by age and curriculum but rather develops from tasks and problems put in place by the teacher. While his views on pedagogy have been subject to significant criticisms, we would argue that a combination of his interpretations of both pedagogy and andragogy can be combined when considering the sorts of homework activities you can do across all age ranges. We also think it is helpful to consider the many roles that a teacher occupies, i.e. that of instructor, guide, facilitator and consultant.

Social constructivist schools of psychology contribute to learning theory and its impact on the sorts of homework teachers can set by focusing on the thinking processes when learning takes place. The constructivist approach is more concerned with processes of learning and the role of the learner in particular and assumes that there is no such thing as 'fact' in that all facts, scientific or otherwise, are socially constructed in the first place. Knowledge is therefore assumed to be constructed by learners themselves and learning is seen as an active process of construction and knowledge accumulation. The teacher is no longer assumed to be the deliverer of knowledge but the facilitator of active learning. Learners 'restructure' what they see and hear and think and rethink ideas until 'personal meanings' are formed. This particular approach to understanding learning assumes that 'mistakes' are 'ok' providing learners 'talk', solve problems, make decisions and form opinions. The teacher is no longer assumed to be the deliverer of knowledge but rather a 'facilitator' of the learners' active learning. Value is therefore placed on homework providing a variety of active learning that learners take up along with the facilitator role that the teacher occupies.

We are conscious, when writing this book, of the interesting possibilities for homework and learning outside of the classroom being opened up by the rapid expansion of new and emerging technologies, Web2.0 tools and social media. We are also conscious, in this new digital landscape, of the importance for homework to be relevant for learners' lives while understanding the serious consequences a digital divide might have on access to homework resources for all. The homework activities generated in this book through the use of digital technologies are sometimes referred to as being 'e-learning'. E-learning often fits into a broader cognitive or constructivist approach described above since it is seen to offer, if done well, (inter)active engagement, learner choice and flexibility. E-learning might involve the use of the internet as a research tool or the interactive smart board as a way to encourage learners to manipulate images and text. As a distinctive theory of learning, many propose that we should seek to 'blend' the traditional and the new – the non-digital and the digital – together. This is seen to maximize the ways we can interact with learners and to motivate learners. It is also seen as a source of differentiation if we can offer different learners a variety of approaches that they can choose from. In this sense, all teaching and learning is 'blended' since most of us choose from the range of theories on offer above and merge many ideas together.

Broadly speaking behaviourist approaches to learning (see: Skinner 1957; Thorndike 1911; Watson 1913) allow for a focus on teacher and learner behaviour. Like Pavlov's (1927) dogs the focus of such approaches considers 'rewards' for learners (e.g. certificates, praise and the speed in which marked work is returned to learners). However, such rewards can also be 'negative' e.g. positioning homework as a punishment for poor behaviour rather than as an opportunity to enhance the educational experience. In contrast to social constructivism, behaviourist views emphasize a process of knowledge transmission and the expert role allocated to the teacher rather than the learning activities of learners. They also help in emphasizing the importance of the speed with which students are 'rewarded' by homework being marked quickly and with sufficiently structured and guided formative feedback (or 'feedforward').

BEST PRACTICE – IMPLICATIONS FROM RESEARCH INFORMED PRACTICE

- Instructions about homework are often given hurriedly with insufficient guidance and inadequate opportunities to seek clarification.
- Homework is often set 3–4 minutes before the end of lessons when many students are packing away and not listening to instructions.
- Only 36 per cent of students in one study (Hallam 2005) reported that teachers 'always' mark their work.
- Teacher feedback is seen as crucial in improving attainment and in motivating students to do homework.
- There is a point at which more time on homework has a negative effect on learning.
- The longer the return of marked homework to students the less effective it is as a form of assessment.

Ongoing research on 'multiple intelligences', famously encapsulated by the work of American psychologist Howard Gardner, has significantly informed many of the homework strategies in this book. Rather than having an intelligence defined by somebody's 'IQ', Gardner (1993) argues that humans are better thought of as having nine or more intelligences, the most significant being the following:

- Linguistic – the ability to learn, explore, play and develop language or languages;
- Logical/mathematical – the ability to excel in mathematical problem solving or lateral thinking;
- Musical – the ability to recall music (be it pitch, rhythm or timbre) on first hearing and/or the ability to 'naturally' pick up a musical instrument and play melodies without instruction. The ability to listen to, and discern differences in, a variety of musical styles;
- Spatial – the ability to map read, recall and describe places by picturing them in your mind and perhaps the ability to conceptualize thoughts in diagrammatical form. The ability to re-create visual experience;

- Bodily Kinaesthetic – as exemplified by athletes, dancers and other physical performers, this refers to the ability to control and orchestrate bodily motions along with the ability to handle objects skilfully (e.g. jugglers and footballers);
- Naturalist – the most recent of Gardner's intelligences, this refers to the ability to recognize and categorize natural objects;
- Interpersonal – the ability to read other people's moods, feelings and motivations and other mental states;
- Intrapersonal – the ability to access one's own moods, feelings and motivations and draw on them to guide behaviour;
- Existential – the ability to raise fundamental questions about existence, life, death and finitude.

Humanistic approaches (e.g. Froebel 1900; Montessori 1909; Rogers 1969) to education focus on the importance of meeting the emotional and developmental needs of learners. The role that emotions play in the classroom is stressed under this approach with greater emphasis on personal rather than purely intellectual development. Much importance is placed on the holistic development of the individual including their emotional growth. This approach views learners as being afforded the opportunity to pursue their own interests within a non-threatening environment. Carl Rogers (1969) typifies this particular philosophy arguing that learning will occur when the educator acts as a facilitator by establishing an atmosphere in which learners feel comfortable to consider new ideas and do not feel threatened. Rogers argues that:

- Human beings have a natural eagerness to learn.
- Facilitative teachers are less protective of their constructs and beliefs than other teachers.
- They listen to their learners, especially to their feelings.
- They pay as much attention to their relationship with learners as to the content of the course.
- They can accept constructive feedback (both positive and negative) and use it to add further insight into themselves and their behaviour.
- Learners should be encouraged to take responsibility for their own learning.
- Learners should provide much of the input for the learning which occurs through their insights and experiences.
- They should be encouraged to consider that the most valuable form of evaluation is self-evaluation.
- Learning needs to focus on factors that contribute to solving significant problems or achieving significant results.

This humanistic emphasis on the importance of emotions in successful learning and the strategies teachers can use for homework is backed up by more recent neuroscientific research. Frank McNeil (1999) has written extensively about brain research and learning and argues that the young brain develops at an astonishing rate in response to streams of information via the senses of touch, smell, taste, hearing, sight and bodily movement. He argues that this illustrates how the young mind can sustain concentration when the learning environment and tasks in hand are very carefully structured with these senses in mind. By the time the adult brain reaches maturity it contains over 100 billion brain cells (neurons) and despite popularized thinking about neurological development ceasing at a particular age, parts of the brain continue to develop throughout our adult lives complementing notions of lifelong learning in all disciplines (Glick 2006). The generation of certain chemicals responsible for transmission of information from one neuron to the next (neurotransmitters) is vital to the learning process (Howard-Jones 2002). From a neurological perspective, a sense of excitement and novelty in homework activities can help to generate dopamine, a neurotransmitter that creates a feeling of well-being. This, in turn, helps reinforce the particular learning experience taking place at the time and the way information is transmitted from one neuron to the next. Conversely, unstimulating homework tasks can generate other neurotransmitters (serotonin and cortisol) which decrease attention and learning. Once released into our bodies, these two particular chemicals can inhibit learning from taking place (LeDoux 2002) and subsequently reduce the efficacy of homework activities.

LINKING THEORY WITH PRACTICE

The current renaissance of educational interest in neuroscience and the ways in which this relatively new discipline can shed light on how we develop and learn has had a significant boost from the work of Andrew Pollard, Paul Howard-Jones and his colleagues working on the Teaching and Learning Research Programme (James and Pollard 2006). By examining many of the chemical and biological processes behind teaching and learning their work provides an essential platform to re-think and re-evaluate many of the received wisdoms and myths that have dominated educational thinking in the twentieth century. As part of your own professional development see how their ideas can inform your own understanding of teaching and learning and the role that homework plays in these processes.

When considering the role that homework can play in reinforcing learners' existing knowledge and understanding it is also worth reflecting on the work of Dennison and Kirk (1990). They refer to a 'Do, Review, Learn, Apply' learning cycle in which an activity is undertaken (DO) by learners who exercise choice in planning their approach. This is followed by a process of reflection and evaluation (REVIEW). Learners monitor their progress and review their learning and planning in terms of goals, strategies, feelings, outcomes and context. As a result a meaning or hypothesis is formed (LEARN). New insights and understandings are noted and factors that have influenced progress are identified with new strategies devised for further enquiry. This then allows for the planning of future action (APPLY) in light of any new understanding achieved. This model suggests that when structuring homework activities, a teacher can call upon some of the concepts above to incorporate the more reflective and evaluative traits associated with academic success.

Linking homework to the curriculum

The above phrase is rather curious – why wouldn't homework be linked to the curriculum? How could it not be? But the thing is, as teachers we need to demonstrate to learners precisely how homework is linked to their learning and lessons. We already know that this is important from the work conducted into AfL (see Chapter 5): learners need to understand how and why their learning 'fits in'. In other words the connections between lessons, tasks, learning activities, assessment and lesson aims and objectives need to be made clear so that learners can understand the point they are at in their learning journey and where they would be going to next. We believe the same about homework. It needs to be connected and entrenched into normal and usual classroom routines. One reason why some learners fail to complete homework (or fail to do it at a meaningful level of engagement) is that it appears disjointed or unconnected from lessons themselves (see Chapters 2 and 7). For example, putting homework collection and announcements at the end of a lesson might make it look like an afterthought. Worse still, some teachers, pushed for time, rush homework announcements at the end of lessons. Think what is actually being communicated here. Equally, by having homework set at the end of the lesson – after the 'taught' lesson – places homework in a subservient role to classroom teaching; it always comes after. Thus the next lesson (where homework is due in) is something new; learners and teachers have moved on. And the previous week's homework is now 'old news' – something lagging behind.

Given the above, we suggest that the following re-conceptualization of homework is needed:

- Homework links into the themes, aims and objectives of the lesson it is due in; such homework becomes meaningful if learners can be directed to see the purpose of the work and how it connects to future learning.
- Homework needs to inform the lesson content – right from the 'starter' to the lesson onwards. In this way homework becomes directly linked to the curriculum and to the learning journey – rather than piecemeal, an add-on.

To help inform this HfL approach, we use the following icon ⓕ in Chapter 7 to flag up to you when a homework strategy is especially suited as a starter activity. This should help you to start to build clear links between the homework you set and the lesson planning you are doing. Making learners see the value of the homework and other learning outside of the classroom is the key to this HfL approach, and as such the key to ensuring learners will complete homework in a timely and meaningful fashion.

> **FREQUENTLY ASKED QUESTIONS – HOW MUCH TIME SHOULD LEARNERS SPEND ON HOMEWORK?**
>
> The literature on homework and the ideal time spent on activities varies enormously making it impossible to recommend with authority ideal times. Too many variables (e.g. age, gender, location, subject discipline, type of school, availability of resources and so on) complicate any meaningful generalization. However in talking to school leaders and examining school policies the following times would appear to be common-place:
>
> | | |
> |---|---|
> | Years 7–8 (11–13-year-olds): | 45 to 90 minutes per day |
> | Year 9 (13–14-year-olds): | 60 to 120 minutes per day |
> | Years 10–11 (14–16-year-olds): | 90 to 150 minutes per day |
> | Year 12 onwards (16 years plus): | up to 180 minutes per day |

Homework and curriculum planning

How much or how little time learners should spend on homework is a debate that teachers, parents, politicians and educational leaders have struggled with since the formation of formal education. Susan Hallam (2005) reminds us that since the nineteenth century homework has been used to supplement the curriculum and has been fashionable or not, depending on political, social, economic and educational factors. When concern is raised about falling educational standards, she argues, the amount of homework set by schools tends to increase but when pressure on children and family life becomes intolerable campaigners for the well-being of children call for its reduction. As with most things in education successful homework strategies depend on careful planning by teachers, managers and school/college leaders. This planning needs to consider the formal, informal and extra-curricular activities that learners of all ages engage with. One starting point is to ensure that each institution has a meticulously constructed homework policy ensuring that all teachers are aware of its existence and content. Two factors are crucial in underpinning successful homework policies:

1. They guarantee that all tasks set appropriate for the learner's age and ability.
2. They carefully consider the learner's other commitments (e.g. responsibilities at home, part-time employment, hobbies, sport and so on).

Many homework policies will spell out, for the benefit of parents/guardians, learners and teachers, the purposes of homework. Typically these will be:

1. to improve, consolidate and reinforce skills and understanding in the core subjects of literacy and numeracy, as well as other areas of curriculum when appropriate;
2. to both reinforce and extend understanding, as fits the needs of the learner;
3. to build on achievement in the classroom/studio/workshop;
4. to support the development of independent study skills;
5. to develop an effective partnership between home and school/college, providing parents/guardians with the opportunity to be involved in the learner's education.

All subject departments should clearly communicate in their homework policy:

- when homework will be set;
- how much homework should be set;
- types of homework used;
- place of homework in the scheme of work;
- sanctions for unsatisfactory work;
- how and by whom homework will be monitored;
- homework action plan following most recent detailed monitoring of homework.

How schools and colleges construct and facilitate their homework policy will vary from institution to institution and will reflect the values of its leaders and managers. However in formulating that policy the following points should be carefully considered and communicated to teachers:

- the importance of success criteria;
- the range of activities and tasks that set for students of differing ages and abilities;
- the amount and frequency of homework set for different ages;
- how homework tasks can be differentiated;
- how homework should be marked and assessed and how homework success can be rewarded (e.g. communicating with parents/guardians, awarding of certificates);
- how non-completion of homework should be dealt with.

Conclusion

In the later chapters of this book we unite the claims of educational theory, the research that underpins it, and the best practice we have observed in our roles as teachers and teacher educators. We hope that you enjoy and find useful the ideas in this book and the 300 homework strategies we suggest, remembering that teachers are learners too! We would therefore urge you to reflect upon what you are doing, why you are doing it and how best you can improve your own practice and the practice of all your learners.

QUESTIONS FOR PROFESSIONAL DEVELOPMENT

1. What are your colleagues' views on homework as a strategy for teaching and learning and in what ways do their thoughts influence your own professional values?
2. In what ways can the educational theories discussed in this chapter assist in planning, facilitating and evaluating the homework activities you create for your learners?
3. In what ways can you incorporate recent developments in neuroscience into the implementation and evaluation of your own ideas of teaching, learning and homework?
4. Do you keep any sort of professional reflective journal? If not then we would suggest that you create one to use as you work through the ideas in this book. By reflecting on your own professional practice you will be able to quickly determine which ideas work and why and embed these ideas in your own professional philosophy and practice.

2 Why they will always do your homework

Chapter objectives

In this chapter we will:

- explore the relationship between homework, planning and teaching and learning;
- introduce strategies to ensure completion of homework;
- discuss a variety of ways that parents can be involved in strategies for learning outside the classroom;
- examine best practice when working with other colleagues.

Introduction – 'It's not worth not doing it'

Research in recent years has indicated that teacher expectations are the singularly most powerful factor in determining whether or not learners will regularly complete homework activities (Hallam 2005; Muis and Reynolds 2011). This has enormous implications for your own practice and the ways in which you communicate your expectations to your learners about the role you believe homework can play in raising their achievement, enjoyment and motivation. While a variety of factors lie beyond your control in determining whether homework is completed (e.g. family pressures, lack of resources and so on) there is much you can do – must do – to convince your learners that homework must always be done for you (e.g. by not setting homework within the last couple of minutes of your lesson when attention levels are low and so on). This is vital because the message that homework is relatively unimportant to some teachers will quickly worm its way back to learners, their parents/guardians and future cohorts of learners making it almost impossible to re-establish good practice. How you convey this along with your determination to ensure that all work you set is completed will not only raise achievement levels with your learners but also mark you out as an exceptional practitioner in their eyes. In this chapter we introduce you to a variety of ideas related to planning, research, theory and good practice that will ensure that your learners will value the work you set and think twice before considering whether or not they should skip it.

BEST PRACTICE – ALWAYS DO WHAT YOU SAY YOU WILL DO!

Really effective teachers working in schools and colleges use a variety of strategies to ensure that the homework they set is always completed and completed on time. These include:

- firmly embedding homework strategies by tackling non-completers early on;
- discussing with them why the work has not been done and negotiating a new deadline with action promised if the deadline is missed;
- where appropriate phoning parents/guardians when work is not completed;
- being 100 per cent consistent in collecting in work at the agreed time/place;
- not setting homework in the final few minutes of the lesson;
- providing clear instructions, advice and guidance so that there is no reason why the work cannot be carried out by the learner;
- using institutional procedures (e.g. contacting tutors, year heads etc.) if the work persistently is not carried out.

LINKING THEORY WITH PRACTICE

In Chapter 1 we looked at educational theories and their relationship to teaching and learning outside of the classroom. As teachers we can combine different pedagogic approaches and teaching strategies in interesting ways when thinking about homework and other issues of learning and teaching. So we can, for example, think about homework from both a behaviourist and an A4L position at the same time. Think carefully about how long it takes you to mark and return homework and the feedback that you write. Remember that behaviourist approaches to education (see Chapter 1) acknowledge the importance of rapid feedback on any assessment when motivating learners. Feedback (or 'feedforward') needs to acknowledge and praise any particular strengths while clearly signposting for learners how they can improve their work in the future. The longer it takes for work to be marked and returned to students the less motivated they will be to do work of a similar standard in future.

Lesson planning and schemes of work

We have argued elsewhere (Kidd and Czerniawski 2010) that the best lessons are performances that are meticulously planned, scripted and resourced. Underpinning these performances – like any good play or piece of theatre – is time spent planning and preparing. This is the hidden work of all good teachers; 'hidden' in the sense that we see the results – the classroom practice – but often are unaware until we enter the profession just what this means in terms of work and effort. Meticulous planning of what, how and when homework is set is crucial to the success of your teaching. So too is how that homework is used and followed up in the classroom as part of the learning and assessment process.

Most lesson planning takes two forms: the individual lesson plans of the teacher and the scheme of work (SOW) that the lesson plans draw upon. While these documents (see Table 2.1 and Table 2.2) are important for the self-assessment, monitoring and quality assurance for the institution in which you practise, they are equally important to ensure that colleagues, learners (and parents) do not get snowed under with an avalanche of homework (and marking) all at the same time.

Table 2.1 Section of typical lesson plan identifying homework to be collected and set

LESSON PLAN			
Topic		Programme of study	
Teaching Group:	Date:	Lesson time & duration:	No. of pupils:
National Curriculum Attainment target level (if relevant):			
Aim of Lesson:			
Learning Objectives		Assessment of Objectives	
Cross-curricular expectations (Literacy, numeracy, citizenship):			
Differentiation and role of additional adults if applicable:			
Subject specific language/key words:		Homework to be collected	
		Homework to be set	

Table 2.2   Section of typical SOW identifying homework to be collected and set

Departmental Scheme of Work					
Week No	Aims	Content	Resources	Functional skills	Homework
Week 1.					
Week 2.					

The distinction between these two documents is:

- **Lesson plans** are individual moments in time; each specific and 'discrete' lesson drawn from the wider picture offered on the scheme of work. Table 2.1 shows the first part of a typical lesson plan highlighting what homework needs to be set and whether or not homework should be collected.
- **Schemes of work (SOW)** represent the larger picture; a series of lessons matching together and making up, over time, the whole course of learning for a year, a module or a term (depending how these are organized within the institution in question). In Table 2.2, homework is included as a category that can be easily identified for internal (e.g. teachers, line managers, etc.) and external (e.g. inspectors, governors, etc.) auditing purposes.

Although schemes of work are planned before individual lesson plans – this is probably not going to be the case for the experience of many student teachers or those qualified joining new institutions. In both cases you will join an institution 'already in motion' with planning for the year largely set before you arrive. Allow your colleagues and mentor to guide you, but always keep in mind that homework needs to be strategically placed for its successful implementation. Homework policies in schools and colleges vary but might include specific days of the week for collecting homework or where homework is set per subject e.g. Mondays: French and mathematics; Tuesdays: business studies and so on. In planning for homework and designing schemes of work consider the following points:

1. **Institutional procedures** Do college/school regulations specify a maximum time spent on homework? Are schools and colleges able to support, with resources, the completion of homework, for example, library access, homework clubs, quiet work rooms, break-out rooms for communal working and so on?
2. **Team teaching** Avoid setting homework at the same time as other colleagues in your team.
3. **Skills development** What are the subject's foundation skills and how might these best be targeted as the year progresses?
4. **Assessment** When and how will learners be formally and informally assessed and how can homework support the process (e.g. the use of homework in public

examination revision)? How does homework fit within your emerging philosophy of assessment (e.g. what emphasis do you give on formative, summative and ipsative assessment strategies)?

?

FREQUENTLY ASKED QUESTIONS – WHAT IS THE DIFFERENCE BETWEEN 'FORMATIVE', 'SUMMATIVE' AND 'IPSATIVE' ASSESSMENT?

We cover this in more detail in Chapter 5 but formative assessment refers to any type of assessment that takes place during the programme of study that informs the future progress of the learner. It is ongoing, not final. It is used to check progress and to support further development. Summative assessment is any type of assessment that usually occurs at the end of the programme of study and is a final measurement of the outcome of the programme being studied. Having said this, it can also provide a 'snapshot' of the progress of the learner at any given point during the course (e.g. tests, exams or even on the spot direct questioning of a learner). Ipsative assessment usually refers to a process of learner self-assessment; the learner identifies their own position within their learning and assesses their own needs. This assessment method is often about the 'distance travelled' as identified by the learner themselves. It can happen entirely separately from the role or input of a teacher, as well as being supported 'from the side' by a teacher or another learner. Thinking about homework strategies within these three categories really helps when planning and evaluating activities and the relationship they have to the assessment of learning.

---

5. **Holidays** How will holiday periods impact on the nature and size of the work set?
6. **Motivating learners** What sorts of activities capture the interest of your learners and how might these increase motivation and enjoyment of the subject?
7. **Teacher expectation** Identify your expectations for all learners including those who might attain levels above and below the required level.
8. **Differentiation of learners** What sorts of activities address each of your learners' needs and provide you with invaluable assessment information to stretch and challenge all learners?

As you develop your homework strategies consider and reflect on the following questions:

- Should you set a certain amount of time to be spent on homework and accept that different learners will produce different amounts?
- Should you set a task knowing that it will take learners different amounts of time to complete?

- What sorts of strategies do you have in place for when learners fail to hand work in on time?
- How and when should you collect homework in?

It is also important for you, as a professional, to develop your own emerging philosophy about homework around these questions, approaching schemes of work with a degree of flexibility. Having said this, you still need to ensure that all aspects of the programme are covered and that all learners have been stretched to the best of their ability – and are then moved forward.

LINKING THEORY WITH PRACTICE

Many teachers find engaging in action research helpful and productive. The idea is that you identify from your own reflective work an aspect of your practice that you wish to improve and you then go about an enquiry based upon this practice: you experiment, review the outcomes and find new and more profitable ways of working. Implementing new homework strategies and then studying their outcomes would make a great basis for an action research project. Introduced in team meeting agendas or as a topic for whole institutional meetings new strategies could be introduced and then carefully monitored to see what improvements could be made at individual, team and institutional levels.

BEST PRACTICE – HOMEWORK AS STARTER ACTIVITIES

Part 2 of the book contains 300 homework ideas and we have highlighted many of those that can be used to create starters activities for your lessons. Homework completion rates can be boosted significantly if learners see the relationship between homework and classroom tasks. The starts of lessons are ideal for this particularly if those activities involve learners working together, e.g. through the creation of quizzes, bringing in artefacts, taking pictures, etc. Assessment can be strengthened when combined with effective questioning strategies by the teacher to ensure that tasks have been carried out successfully.

Strategies for dealing with non-completion of homework

While there is much that you can do to raise expectations and the importance of homework in the eyes of your learners we also accept that most successful institutions are ones where there is considerable inter-departmental coordination and discussion about the purpose, timing, level of difficulty, availability of resources and range of activities associated with homework. Evidence suggests that teachers' beliefs about attitudes towards homework differ depending on whether the school/college where they are employed has a clear policy on homework and supports it being set (Hallam 2005). In a study by MacBeath and Turner (1990) learners interviewed in their study maintained that homework should be:

- directly related to the work carried out in school/college;
- structured, logical and strategically beneficial to their learning needs;
- wide ranging in terms of the activities set;
- doable but sufficiently challenging;
- capable of acknowledging the creativity of the learner;
- capable of enhancing comprehension and self-confidence;
- acknowledged and rewarded;
- guided and supported.

We would argue that if these principles are adopted as those that underpin your practice then you will be that teacher that learners prioritize over others when they do their homework.

Sometimes however it is not possible, despite all our best intentions, for some learners to carry out homework tasks. Table 2.3 indicates more common reasons why students find completing homework difficult and offers some initial diagnostic solutions.

Many teachers view homework as something that reinforces, reviews, and practises the content/concepts/theories, etc. taught in their lessons. The nature and the presentation of the task will significantly affect to what extent learners believe that the work set is useful to them. When considering your own practice reflect on the following three questions:

1. Do all learners get the sense that any activity they are doing is more than just a 'finishing-off' activity and one that will actively enhance their understanding of the subject as a whole?
2. Will the work they produce be useful for them when they need to revise for future exams?
3. Is the work likely to be quickly marked and with suitable guidance on how learners can improve their work in future?

How you reflect on these three questions has implications for the sorts of resources you design, the skills you may need to develop and apply and the ways in which the tasks are scaffolded for your learners. For example, do your learners get a sense that the resources you produce for homework activities match the pride and presentation skills you adopt when teaching in-class activities? Are the tasks you set fully utilizing your skills on Word? For example are there diagrams, blank boxes, arrows, borders, etc. on the worksheets you produce? Do you photocopy these onto coloured paper to make them more engaging and

Table 2.3 Common reasons for non-completion of homework

Common reasons for non-completion of homework	Strategies to encourage homework completion
Lack of motivation	• Tasks need to be engaging, 'doable', and relevant to the learner • Talk with the learner, parent/guardian about reasons for lack of motivation • Ensure 'carrot and stick' strategies are always carried out when promised (e.g. praise to parents, detentions, letters home, etc.)
Insufficient time	• Check SOWs and liaise with colleagues as to how much/when homework is set and by whom • Ensure that tasks are 'doable' within reasonable timeframes • Provide information about homework clubs, access to classrooms before/end of school/college day, etc. • Provide homework diaries/timetables and sit down with learners to discuss organization skills
Lack of resources	• Ensure that homework is 'doable' for all learners (i.e. that the work does not require resources that some might not have (e.g. video cameras, laptops, etc.) • Supply, where necessary, relevant resources or indicate where these can be obtained (e.g. library, homework club, etc.) • Set paired homework so that resources can be shared • Create a 'resource' bank
Misunderstanding tasks set	• Set instructions for homework early in the lesson and ensure that all are listening • Back up spoken instructions with written (on smart board, whiteboard, hand out, etc.) • Get students in pairs to confirm understanding • Ensure no impediment to learning (e.g. eyesight, hearing, etc.)
Lack of sufficient study area at home	• Introduce learners to homework club, library, etc. • 'model' good practice by providing diagrams/pictures, etc. of suitable working environment and create similar in classroom • Regularly check folders/books, etc. to emphasize importance of organizational skills • Talk to parents/guardians about suitable working environments (e.g. desk layout, folders, suitable shelf-space, use of local library, etc.)
Family responsibilities	• Sensitively talk to learner and if necessary contact family about possible solutions, agreements, alternative deadlines, etc. • Negotiate early/late entry to school/college with supervision if necessary • Liaise with other staff to ensure learner is not vulnerable to dangerous influences from adults, peer groups, etc.

easier to file and revisit? Can tasks be accessed and read by all? Can they be read on any digital device? Are they uploaded into your VLE (Virtual Learning Environment)? Addressing these questions and acting upon them will significantly raise learner expectations about the priority you place on the purpose of homework for learner engagement and achievement.

Think carefully about why you set homework and when. Some teachers make the mistake of setting homework as a punishment: 'If you do this again you will do extra homework on...' Comments like this undermine the creativity and curiosity that many homework activities can engender, reducing homework to a chore rather than a valued learning opportunity. Many teachers often set homework hurriedly within the last three to four minutes of the lesson and in many cases after the lesson has ended. Instructions are often rushed and unclear. It is therefore little surprise that many young people leave the room ill informed and with little sense of the importance of the work they have to do. Added to this a significant amount of homework carried out by students is left unmarked and this can demoralize and demotivate many learners who initially might be very enthusiastic to engage in the tasks set by teachers, particularly at the start of a course, year, term, etc. We have argued elsewhere (Kidd and Czerniawski 2011) for the importance of formative assessment and how good feedback is better expressed as 'feed-forward' when engaging and motivating teenage learners. Evidence suggests that multiple feedback with marks/grades, targets, evaluative comments and explanations on how work can be improved, is a significant factor raising the importance of homework in the eyes of learners (Hallam 2005). This can be done in a variety of ways and we address this in Chapter 5.

Consider the following strategies for preventing the non-completion of homework:

- Create a homework league table and offer a prize at the end of each half term for the top three learners.
- Coordinate homework with other teachers/departments (refer to your schemes of work).
- Be meticulous in recording what homework was set and when in your mark book/assessment records.
- Photocopy the occasional page of homework to send home to parents/guardians.
- Make sure that all homework activities are seen by learners as relevant, useful and doable.
- If appropriate do not be afraid to ring parents/guardians about homework. Many parents value the opportunity to speak with teachers and you will quickly get a reputation with learners as a result.
- Monitor homework diaries and make sure you are in regular contact with tutors/year heads/faculty managers, etc. keeping them informed.
- Refer to outside/interested bodies regarding specific deadline dates (parents evenings, reports, exam boards).
- Make sure that you do what you say you do – e.g. in schools if you set a detention because of lack of homework, then give it.

- Make sure homework instructions are not left until the last minute and that learners write down these instructions (or that they are written down for them).
- Offer prizes for the best homework.
- Contact form tutors/heads of year immediately that a pattern of non-completion starts to emerge.
- Explain clearly sanction procedures and follow them rigidly.
- Offer learners an option/choice if homework is not done before a penalty is given e.g. 'get it to me by Thursday or you have 1000 word essay on…', etc.
- Give clear and slow instructions (vocal and written) when launching homework tasks.
- Do not give homework at the end of a lesson.
- Mark all work regularly and return quickly with clear advice/guidance/targets.
- Create templates/proformas for marking homework to minimize marking time and emphasize the skills domains associated with the subject.
- Refer learners as and when necessary to homework clubs.
- Involve learning assistants/learning mentors in the design, setting and collection of homework.
- Offer learners a choice of activities (this could be linked to any evaluation you might have carried out about favourite types of homework, learning styles, etc.).

> **BEST PRACTICE – S.M.A.R.T AND R.U.M.B.A**
>
> Two acronyms that many experienced teachers use when planning and facilitating tasks, including setting homework, are S.M.A.R.T (Specific, Measurable, Achievable, Relevant, Timed) and R.U.M.B.A (Relevant, Understandable, Measurable, Behavioural, Achievable). Both acronyms offer invaluable 'check lists' when setting homework tasks that can be realistically carried out while still providing sufficient academic challenge. If homework completion rates are less than satisfactory it might be worth contemplating whether or not the tasks you set and the instructions that accompany them adhere to all component parts of these two acronyms.

Getting parents involved

Parents often have mixed feelings about homework and the effects it has on their children and family life in general. While most parents appreciate the benefits that regular homework has on educational achievement and expect it to play a significant role in the educational process, time spent on homework can impact on household chores, hobbies and communal family life. Many parents feel that quite often homework is poorly set, inadequately marked and lacking in meaningful interaction between learner and teacher in terms of the usefulness of the feedback (Hallam 2004). Research has shown how teachers often find themselves caught between conflicting expectations about what 'good' homework is and these expectations can vary depending on whether they come from the government, the institution, parents or teachers (Czerniawski 2011). There can, for example, be a discrepancy between what parents consider to be appropriate homework tasks (e.g. essays, note taking, presentation preparation, etc.) and what some teachers might consider to be more exciting tasks (e.g. making pod-casts, taking photos, constructing lyrics to songs, etc.).

As experienced teachers ourselves, we recognize how homework can often be a site of anxiety between parents and many teenagers. Many researchers (e.g. Soloman et al. 2002; Walker et al. 2004) argue that homework can have a negative impact on family life adding to the tensions that already exist in some families. These tensions can be exacerbated when some parents view homework as an opportunity for their children to make up for failures they experienced when they were learners. Many parents may believe that they lack sufficient knowledge, skills and time to be able to support their children and feel alienated from their learners and the teachers that teach them. Some parents, depending on their cultural and socio-economic background, will find the process of supporting their children in homework tasks difficult. Some teachers can misinterpret this lack of parental involvement as a lack of interest. Such misinterpretations can be further exacerbated if parents do not attend parents' evenings when in reality such evenings can be intimidating for those parents who lack the linguistic or cultural capital required to successfully negotiate these meetings. It is therefore incredibly important that teachers are sensitive to this when considering how best homework can be used to support learner development and the ways in which this is communicated to the parents/guardians of the young people they teach.

> **BEST PRACTICE – TEXT MESSAGING PARENTS AND STUDENTS**
>
> Many schools and colleges use text messaging services (SMS) to contact parents about the progress of their children. This can be used to inform parents about events, absenteeism, deadlines and any non-completed work. Group messages can also be sent to learners' mobile phones as deadline reminders for coursework, etc.

In recent years there has been an increasing emphasis on encouraging parents to become involved in the education of their children (Hallam 2005). Research has shown that parental support and involvement in homework can be extremely beneficial with higher rates of completion and fewer problems experienced by learners when engaging in tasks (Patell et al. 2009). This works best when parents show an interest in the task being done, encourage their children to complete activities and provide a routine as to when activities need to be carried out. Advice on time management and organizational skills can be invaluable. The trick, however, is to pull all of this off with teenagers who may, or may not, appreciate such advice and guidance.

If at all possible, talk to parents (parents evenings in schools and colleges are great for this) and try to find out whether or not their children have the right sort of working conditions they require to carry out study at home. Offer alternatives, e.g. homework clubs, library space, early arrival and use of classroom space, etc. Find out what the school/college homework policy is and talk this through with parents. Schemes of work can be simplified and sent to parents so that they are aware of homework tasks and deadlines. Homework schedules can be printed onto stickers with a space for parents to sign when each piece of work is completed. If necessary devise a 'homework guidance sheet' for parents to include the following:

- learner responsibility re: homework (e.g. deadlines, presentation, etc.);
- what is expected from parents/guardians regarding homework, e.g. checking that the work is done;
- parental signing of homework diaries;
- the role of parental praise, etc.;
- how the nature of homework will change as learners progress through the year at school/college;
- the ideal working environment (e.g. computer; ventilation; heating; bookshelves; lack of distraction, etc.);
- advice/guidance on time management.

Quite often parents comment on the fact that the only time that teachers contact them is when poor behaviour or poor performance become an issue. Wouldn't it be lovely if more teachers rang, emailed or sent notes/cards home that praised learners about the work they have done? If you do this you will gain the respect of parents and learners and reinforce all teaching and learning strategies you deploy.

Working with other colleagues

Working in isolation is never fun and the best departments in schools and colleges are those that work closely together. Meetings in such departments can be invaluable in sharing good practice about teaching in general and homework ideas in particular. Meetings can also be used to moderate the marking of particular homework tasks to ensure consistency in assessment. Many successful departments in schools and colleges make a point of sharing good practice as the first item on any meeting agenda. Administrative issues can dominate meeting agendas leaving the sharing of good practice to a rushed discussion at the end. Increasingly common are so-called 'learning lounges' where groups of professionals come together to share good practice free from the administrative constraints that dominate more formal meetings.

Schemes of work are often written by heads of departments or leading practitioners whose experience is often seen as the most efficient means by which these documents are written. While this is understandable it makes more sense to draw together a variety of practitioners in the planning process prior to the writing of these important documents. By doing this homework activities can be carefully woven into the overall big picture of how a particular unit/module, etc. can be best delivered drawing on the expertise of a variety of practitioners. For example teaching assistants and Special Educational Needs Coordinators (SENCOs) can be consulted as to how, when and under what circumstances certain tasks can best be supported. Teaching assistants can be deployed in the classroom to support, monitor and collect homework raising their status and importance in the eyes of young learners.

Virtual Learning Environments (VLEs) are increasingly being used in schools and colleges for a variety of purposes. Colleagues can use these to coordinate and display homework tasks and deadline dates and allow learners' parents to have access to these. Staffroom notice boards in many schools and colleges use display boards with planners highlighting what homework tasks have been set and by whom. Careful coordination of these dates can result in an easier workload for teacher and learner alike without sacrificing learning outcomes. Similarly such tracker charts can display the names of all learners and allow teachers to sign off completed homework tasks. Form tutors and subject teachers can then instantly identify those learners not completing work. Such information can be invaluable for future planning and, in some cases, can be really helpful in identifying learners who may be encountering personal problems that otherwise might have gone unnoticed.

Identifying cross-curricular links between different subject areas can be an invaluable way to coordinate homework activities across different departments. This has the advantage of sharing the responsibility of generating and collecting homework activities while simultaneously conveying the importance and relationship of these activities to learners. Project competitions can then be arranged between classes with prizes being awarded for the particular class that consistently produces the best work. If appropriate, subject teachers from different subject disciplines can come together to generate universal mark schemes.

Conclusion

In recent years action research for educational practitioners has risen to the fore as a means through which teachers can critically investigate and explore their own practice (see Baumfield et al. 2008), the idea being that schools and colleges are places or communities of learning at every level and that, therefore, teachers within the same learning institutions are members of a 'community of practice' (Lave and Wenger 1991). The adoption of new homework strategies could be the source of experimentation along the lines of practitioner action research. Working with your colleagues you could set a schedule to experiment with different homework strategies and log what you think the outcomes are. If you do this, try to involve the voice of the learners in providing you with feedback on what they thought worked.

QUESTIONS FOR PROFESSIONAL DEVELOPMENT

1. In light of the ideas discussed in this chapter in what ways can you enhance your homework strategies? Revisit your schemes of work and see how you can restructure them in ways that maximize the effectiveness of the homework you set.
2. Go through all the current resources you use and look closely at the homework activities you have set. Focusing on the design/look of the homework tasks you produce in what ways can you produce more engaging and visually appealing resources? Examine all the features on Word to see which ones you could easily adopt when designing your next homework activity.
3. To what extent do you involve other colleagues you work with when considering the range, type, frequency and challenge in the homework activities you create? Suggest to your colleagues that one of the items on any meeting agenda is a discussion of homework activities, their assessment and moderation.
4. When was the last time that you contacted parents to praise their children's work? Build into your schedule a variety of ways in which you can inform parents when your learners do well in a particular homework activity (e.g. sending post-cards, text messages, etc.).

3 Differentiation and homework

Chapter objectives

In this chapter we will:

- introduce the relationship between homework and differentiation;
- provide strategies for how you can differentiate and personalize homework;
- explore the opportunities homework provides to support more able learners;
- review the opportunities homework provides to challenge learners of all abilities.

Introduction – making learning and teaching 'personal'

In our experience as teachers and teacher educators few things are as misunderstood as differentiation. Put simply, we can make a distinction between differentiation and personalization. Whereas differentiation is about identifying difference and responding to the different needs of different groups of learners, personalization is always about meeting individual needs. In practice, we might argue that personalization is a sub-set of differentiation, or that personalization takes differentiation and focuses right down upon the individual.

A commitment to differentiation then, is a commitment to a three-stage process:

1. the identification of ability and need;
2. structuring work, guidance and support to meet need;
3. moving learners forward – challenging and stretching learners in order to be able to progress.

In the hectic and confusing world of the school, college and the individual classroom sometimes the third point is lost. Differentiation to meet an identified need without moving learners forward misses the point of learning and teaching. In this sense, the 'tail is wagging the dog'. The point of all learning and all work set (homework or otherwise) is to move learning forward. Even if the work is not 'new content' as such, and is a recap, review or revision, the learning is still moving forward. This is an important point – learning and curriculum content are not the same thing. We do not require teachers to 'deliver' material, but rather we require teachers to enable learners to learn. They might be going over old material, but the learning still needs to be moving forward. Given this, a differentiated approach to homework and to other guidance, support and learning outside of the classroom can really benefit learners.

When we talk about differentiation as a profession, we make a classic and oft-used distinction between differentiation *by task* and differentiation *by outcome*. In other words, different learners might do different work and activities (by task) or learners might do the same task and develop different quality outcomes in their individual responses (by outcome). The latter is used the most yet it is less effective. The former – differentiation by task – is much more effective, but is significant in its resourcing, teacher-time and planning implications. Similarly, when learners are given different things to do this needs careful management, guidance and support.

The role of 'choice' in differentiated homework

> **FREQUENTLY ASKED QUESTIONS – 'BUT THEY ALL DO THE SAME EXAM, HOW CAN I GIVE THEM DIFFERENT WORK TO DO?'**
>
> We hear this a lot. Many teachers are worried about the considerable pressures of working towards their learners meeting final formally assessed outcomes – and quite understandably and rightly so. As a consequence some teachers feel that all learners need the *same* work, as they will sit the *same* exam. And yet, the point of giving different and differentiated work is not to separate learners and remove the possibility of successful outcomes. Far from it. The point is to strategically target what learners need to do to move them towards the final outcome. Teachers need to ensure a full coverage of curriculum content, but how learners learn things and what skills they need to prioritize should be targeted on a more individual basis.

When it comes to homework, what can we differentiate? What are the variables/circumstances that we can change, in order to meet individual and group need? One aspect of learning and teaching that can be differentiated and personalized is 'choice'. Choice is an essential element of learning and teaching. Teachers make choices everyday regarding what they do and how they do it. But how often do learners make choices? One differentiated approach to homework (and one way to develop learning resilience and independence) is to encourage and support learners to make appropriate and informed choices. If learners are given a variety of tasks to choose from (or even a variety of means to provide answers and responses) and are supported to reflect upon what would suit their needs then choice differentiation can be achieved through 'choice'. Choice is often not encouraged enough. Many schools and colleges wish to support learners in becoming 'independent learners' (see Chapter 4) and choice in homework is an excellent way to start to do this. Consider the list below:

BEST PRACTICE – 10 OPPORTUNITIES FOR ENCOURAGING 'CHOICE' IN HOMEWORK

Below are 10 ideas for encouraging greater choice in learning and teaching. Teachers can vary the following aspects of homework practice:

1. the choice of task learners receive;
2. the time learners have to complete tasks;
3. the number of tasks learners need to complete;
4. how they encourage some learners to complete extra extension tasks;
5. how they identify and direct different levels of outcome for different individuals;
6. giving learners a choice over the format they present their response in;
7. providing learners with frames, scaffolds or exemplars to support them getting started;
8. encouraging learners to seek support from other staff or peers in the completion of work;
9. offering learners the chance of additional teacher support before the homework deadline and early informal feedback;
10. allowing some learners to draw support from additional materials to complete the tasks set.

FREQUENTLY ASKED QUESTIONS – WHAT ARE FRAMES, SCAFFOLDS AND EXEMPLARS AND HOW ARE THEY DIFFERENT?

There are many different ways to support learners in 'making a good start' to a given piece of homework. Teachers can provide ready-made materials into which learners write, helping them to structure their thoughts. This is highly effective and avoids learners staring at blank sheets not knowing where to start. This is especially important for homework where the learning might be completed in isolation and certainly without the presence of the teacher for support. Thus the frames and exemplars become the homework support instead. Of these, we have the following:

Exemplars – provide examples of tasks already completed or provide some 'answers' requiring learners to complete the rest. Show them, or 'model' to them, what it should look like.

> *Frames* – often referred to as 'writing frames' these are documents with the elements of answers pre-structured and some aspects of answers pre-written. Thus, learners write into the frame, which supports and guides their answer. They provide the rest of the content but have some modelled to them first.
>
> *Scaffolds* – both exemplars and frames are examples of a wider category known as 'scaffolds'. To scaffold means to provide support step by step within which learning can take place. Learners are not left to it, but their learning is supported and 'held up'. The important thing to remember about scaffolds is that eventually they are *taken away*, and the learning should be able to stand alone. Thus, use frames and exemplars by all means, but remember to move eventually towards learners not needing them.

When we talk about differentiation, we often encourage teachers to think about different tasks or different support for different groups of learners in planning lessons. If this approach is right for learning *inside* the class, then it applies for learning *outside* the class too. In fact, we could make the argument that as the teacher is not present during homework (unlike the classroom) then there is even more reason for homework to be tailored for individual and group need.

Homework as skills development

When planning lessons, we encourage teachers to think about how they might differentiate learning objectives and outcomes as follows:

By the end of this lesson

> . . . *all* learners will have XXX
> . . . *most* learners will have XXX
> . . . *some* learners will have XXX

This differentiated approach can equally and powerfully be applied to homework tasks and materials. Put simply, different learners can do different homework tasks and in doing so use different materials or present work in different ways. But the options need to be there for this to happen. Teachers need to guide, support and direct learners to understand their own learning and to understand why they are being asked to do what they are doing. This is no different from class work – no different from any work.

The implications for the above mean that homework is no longer 'tagged-on at the end' – no longer an afterthought (see also Chapters 1 and 2). Homework needs to be placed at the forefront of planning, as the opportunities it provides are too significant. Elsewhere we have referred to this as a *Homework for Learning* approach (HfL) (see Chapters 1 and 8).

This is a matter of skills development, and using homework to move learning forward by targeting specific skills.

LINKING THEORY WITH PRACTICE

When we talk about skills and skills development, we often refer to the seminal ideas of Bloom (1956) (also see Chapter 8). Bloom, with later additions from other writers such as Krathwohl (Bloom 1956), identified three domains of learning skills: cognitive domain – thinking; psycho-motor domain – physical and 'doing'; affective domain – relationships and working with others. Within each domain, there is a taxonomy – a hierarchical classification of skills in order of potential development from low order to high order. This approach to skills (and even the language of the skills themselves) is actually deeply engrained into most educational systems and certainly into formal examinations. Given this, aligning homework tasks to these skills is highly profitable.

Taking the ideas of Bloom (1956) and later Anderson and Krathwohl (2001) differentiated homework can target gradual and linear skills development. Consider the 'cognitive domain' as outlined below:

Low order
1. Knowledge
2. Comprehension

High order
3. Application
4. Analysis
5. Synthesis
6. Evaluation

Homework tasks can be clearly linked to these skill areas and their development. If you do this, make sure you make this clear to learners. They need to understand what they are doing and why. Again, explaining the rationale behind the homework and the expected learning outcome is as important as explaining the task itself and the deadline. This might mean you need to spend more time going through the homework, supporting it and setting it up, but again this means it is not perceived as an afterthought but as something significant.

The Assessment for Learning (AfL) agenda in the UK (Assessment Reform Group 2002; Black and Wiliam 1998) recommends that aims and objectives of lessons are made clear to learners. This is now almost a 'truism' of practice – so engrained into the culture of schools and colleges that it is. And yet we also need to do the same for homework: to explain to learners what the learning outcomes are. Equally, we need to set different homework, strategically targeted, which develops different skills, and to encourage learners to identify what skills they are working on and when. While we know little about some learners' understanding of homework (Hallam 2005; Warton 2001), we do know that making learning aims and objectives clear is essential for learners to value the work and understand how to complete it. Learners need to see clearly how homework links to their learning.

> **BEST PRACTICE – MAKE IT CLEAR!**
>
> Consider the following ways to make differentiated homework transparent to learners so that they understand what is expected of them when they do their work:
>
> - Colour code worksheets and tasks. Link each to an identified curriculum or subject skill.
> - Make Blooms taxonomy clear to learners. Explain it to them and link it to the final outcomes of the programme of study. Encourage them to think about what skills they are working on and when.
> - Offer learners choice (see discussion above). Encourage and provide formal opportunities in lessons for them to reflect upon their learning and their work and to identify their strengths and areas to be developed.
> - Have regular learning conversations with small groups and individuals about their progression through the homework and within this the development of essential skills. Get learners to understand why you are setting the tasks you are.

Planning for the learning of *all* learners

A key characteristic of an 'outstanding' teacher is that *all* learners are stretched and challenged. Challenging the more able is, however, something that needs to be planned for and not assumed. Many teachers focus differentiation activities on those who might be seen as 'less able', but ignore those who might need stretch and challenge of a different sort. Interestingly, many of the ideas and strategies for the more able apply equally to all learners. If setting different homework for learners who are identified as 'gifted and talented' there are three key areas you might wish to explore in your differentiated materials:

1. Acceleration – covering materials and content quicker, leaving time for...
2. ...increased breadth and depth of subsequent work,
3. ...and time for developing higher order thinking skills.

Again, adopting Bloom's taxonomy across all three domains can help support this. For example, think carefully in your planning about where gifted and talented learners are in their progression and set homework tasks which support higher order Blooms skills.

?

FREQUENTLY ASKED QUESTIONS – WHEN WE SPEAK OF THE 'GIFTED AND TALENTED' (G AND T) WHAT DO WE MEAN?

The term is not as easy to pin down as you might think and has always been relative and normative – linked to the general cohort from which the 'gifted and talented' sample might be drawn. A rough estimate from the UK (although the debate exists elsewhere but is often expressed in different terms) is that G and T learners account for the 'top' 5 per cent of a school or college. They demonstrate this through outcomes, work patterns, motivation and also leadership and independence skills. If we refer to general dictionary definitions, and think about the words,

Gifted = exceptional talent, natural ability

Talented = a natural aptitude or skill

Within this we can see a socio-biological claim of sorts: 'high achieving' learners are 'predisposed' to have the capacity for higher quality outcomes than others. There is considerable debate about this (McGregor 2007).

We must remember that stretch and challenge are relative *and are essential for everyone*. All learners need variety and stretch – but that this would not look the same (and nor would the materials and tasks for homework themselves) across different groups of learners. That being said, we can identify a number of tasks and approaches that might stimulate and motivate different learners of differing abilities and orientations to learning:

- opportunities to manipulate academic and specialist language in tasks and answers;
- opportunities to work through more materials and tasks at a quicker pace;
- opportunities for self-reflection;
- manipulation of evaluation skills;
- being able to synthesize evidence from a variety of sources;
- having extension tasks;
- manipulating a piece of equipment that requires a greater degree of technical skill and know-how;
- working independently;
- developing speculations, hypothesizing and using conjecture;

- using sources (books, texts, websites) which have more complex or difficult language or seem 'older' materials for an older learner;
- working with a medium which is 'harder' to work with;
- using complex diagrams to stimulate and arouse interest;
- negotiating and choosing work, tasks, materials;
- being asked to address probing questions.

Using a rich variety of these approaches will stimulate the interest of gifted and talented learners. In particular, developing the *thinking skills* of all learners will lead to higher quality outcomes. In this approach, philosophically, thinking is seen as a skill and not an 'ability' as such – it is something that everyone can practise and develop. It is something we can do better. Homework provides some interesting opportunities for this. For example, in thinking about what a 'thinking homework' would look like, we can draw upon the work of McGregor (2007) who identifies the following practices for a thinking skills lesson:

- open tasks;
- responses that encourage creativity and imagination;
- tasks which encourage learners to 'think about their thinking' (called 'metacognition') ;
- being able to link ideas together in new and interesting ways;
- assessing what is valuable and useful about ideas;
- posing thought-provoking questions;
- encouraging learners to think through and to argue for views and opinions which are opposite to those they do share;
- encouraging learners to articulate the steps they have taken in arriving at the conclusions they have.

As we have seen above, choice, thinking skills and stretch and challenge are essential for developing learning further. Homework provides excellent opportunities to target these aspects of learning and teaching. For such homework to be effective, you need to really *know your learners*.

How well do you know your learners? Or rather, how well do you know *all* your learners? Are any missed along the way? When encouraging homework to be completed and in supporting learners in a differentiated way, it is important that you identify the range of skills and needs in your groups – not just the top and bottom; not just those in need of more support and those in need of more stretch and challenge. Sometimes those in the middle can become a silent minority. This is especially true if they complete all work, on time and at a fair level of attainment. It is difficult to admit to this, and everyone in the profession would recognize the problems and dangers, and yet when teaching large groups this can be a reality. Homework that is differentiated is a perfect opportunity to redress this imbalance if it exists. Use homework as a means to really engage with learners. You might like to consider the advice below.

> **BEST PRACTICE – ENGAGE EVERYONE!**
>
> Think about adopting some of these strategies so that the silent majority become visible:
>
> 1. Use homework at the start of lessons in class (see Chapters 2 and 7 for a fuller discussion of this). In this way, you get to see what everyone has done and are able to speak about it as you move around the room.
> 2. Set regular conversations with all learners to explore what they are enjoying, finding difficult and what homework and skills tasks they are valuing as part of their own learning.
> 3. At the end of lessons ask learners to write down what homework they have enjoyed, which they have benefited from the most and what they need to do next.
> 4. At the start of the class, engage learners who might be early with conversations about the homework and their progress with it.
> 5. Offer additional support sessions or optional homework clubs.

Many learners will need support with working appropriately and productively on homework and independent work especially if such work is designed to stretch and challenge them. With appropriate support and guidance (see Chapter 6) homework can lead to vital learning progression.

Ability and 'intelligences'

As well as using Bloom, many teachers try and align differentiated tasks in their planning with the ideas of Gardner (1993) on 'multiple intelligences'. For Gardner 'intelligence' can be identified as a complex interplay of nine or more different types of intelligence and not the more classic reduction of intelligence down to 'IQ' or Intelligence Quota (see Chapter 1 for a fuller discussion). The combination and potential to use (or not) both interpersonal and intrapersonal intelligences are what other writers might refer to as 'emotional intelligence'. For example, Goleman (1995) has suggested that teachers need to support learners in working on developing 'personal intelligences' – how they work with others and understand others. Importantly, as part of these personal intelligences, Goleman also identifies motivation and self-regulation. These are especially important for homework if we require learners to be more self-directed and also more independent. The implications of this are that we might need to support learners to develop the required skills and intelligences in order to be able to successfully complete homework. This is a very different positioning of homework and its significance and value. It suggests that learners need to be supported in undertaking homework before some might be able to maximize their learning through it. Again, this is an issue of differentiation. Some learners might be more 'ready' and able to work in a self-regulated way than others.

Alternatives? Flipping the classroom

There is a different relationship between classroom, homework, differentiation and skills development. There is a debate in education developed through the adoption of eLearning and blended learning methodologies and pedagogies referred to as the 'Flipped Classroom' (see also Chapters 5 and 7). In the Flipped Classroom the 'placement' of delivered content – its time and location (and manner of delivery) – is reversed. In the norm, classroom work is about new materials and knowledge supported by the teacher. In these classrooms homework becomes the working through of further examples or demonstrating understanding by completing tasks. This is a bit of a generalization, but this pattern does exist. In the Flipped Classroom, this is turned on its head. Thus, homework is where knowledge is engaged with, researched and explored leaving the classroom freed up for skills development. This is made possible by deploying new technologies. For example, taught content can be recorded in advance (podcasted or videoed) and learners engage with these materials for homework. Classroom work becomes more individualized and differentiated as learners are then guided and supported through their skills development. This is only possible as teaching time is 'freed' from curriculum content. Again, this powerfully positions homework as essential to all learning and directly related to classroom work.

Think about the ways in which homework can 'flip' what happens in the classroom and carefully consider the relationship between homework, classwork and skills development. In thinking about your practice and the decisions you are making about your homework tasks and classroom tasks, try and 'fit' your practice into the boxes in Figure 3.1. Do you see any patterns? Are there particular practices you do most often? If this is the case, do you know why? Do you understand your intentionality? At the end of the day, variety works well in learning and teaching.

Whatever you choose you have a number of decisions to make. Consider Figure 3.1.

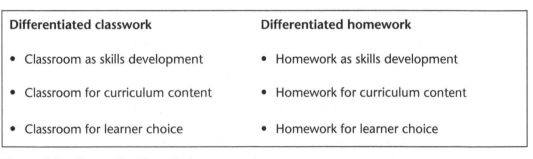

Differentiated classwork	Differentiated homework
• Classroom as skills development	• Homework as skills development
• Classroom for curriculum content	• Homework for curriculum content
• Classroom for learner choice	• Homework for learner choice

Figure 3.1   Choices in differentiation

Conclusion

There is an uncomfortable reality regarding differentiation: while it is essential in moving learning forward, it is often ill considered and not as strategic as it might be. Homework might just be the opportunity to think again about differentiation strategies.

QUESTIONS FOR PROFESSIONAL DEVELOPMENT

1. How might you 'flip your classroom' and rethink the relationship between taught content and homework? What training would you need in learning technologies to support you doing this?
2. To what extent do you think your learners are clear about the learning skills behind the homework you set? Think about how to make work clear.
3. What will you need to do or take out in your lessons to free up time to arrange homework? This will have implications for lesson time and how you might use beginnings and ends of lessons.
4. Do you need to differentiate homework tasks further? What resources will you need to do this?
5. What aspects of your practice do you need to develop as an individual, and what aspects could become a more coordinated and shared strategy between you and other teachers? You might need to seek the support of colleagues and work together to re-think how homework works in your curriculum team. Plan homework and share resources so you can get a sense of the development of the cohort as a whole and not just class by class.

4 Projects, coursework and independent assignments

Introduction – a troubled relationship?

We have all probably seen the news headlines: 'Parents do coursework for children'; 'Learners buy essays from central banks'; 'Coursework is cut and paste from the Internet'. While the events in such news headlines do occur, the extent to which 'cheating' in homework and coursework takes place is unclear. On one hand it might be media exaggeration and moral panic, on the other the tip of a much bigger iceberg. What is clear is that concerns over internet cheating, plagiarism and collaboration and collusion have led to some recent changes to how coursework and project work are perceived in schools and colleges and also in some examples of formal curriculum assessment change. And yet we know that, when entered into correctly, coursework and project and independent assignments for homework – with appropriate guidance and support – can be extremely valuable learning opportunities. Some commentators have already noted that while the quality of classroom based learning and teaching and associated tasks and activities has become more exciting and imaginative over the past few years, the same cannot be said for homework. In some cases homework is becoming 'left behind' even further as the quality of classroom teaching improves (see Henderson 2006). Providing stimulating and well-committed project work supported by appropriate research skills and emerging technologies is a means to bring homework back in line.

In this chapter we explore how to set up, support and maximize opportunities for independent learning over larger, long-term pieces of homework and look at the implications new and emerging technologies might have for homework and independent learning.

Motivating learners

It is certainly the case that longer-term pieces of work can be highly motivating, but the other side of the coin is that without adequate structure and support long-term projects can sometimes feel unwieldy and disconcerting. In the paper *Testing, Motivation and Learning* the Assessment Reform Group (2002) explore the links between motivation, effort and 'motivation for learning' and many of these insights can be applied not just to tests and testing but to longer-term work as well. For example, it is argued that motivation to learn and to complete tasks with confidence is linked to 'self-efficacy' of the learner. This term refers to how one feels able to succeed: at what point do learners feel they need to 'give up'? At what point will learners not undertake tasks as they think they will not be successful in them before they have started? Self-efficacy is also related to the degree to which learners feel that they can direct and take control of the choices in their own learning. Long-term project work and independent work is a golden opportunity for learners to experience the empowerment that choice might bring. Such work offers learners a feeling of 'participation' in their own learning. As Leach and Moon (2008) argue, learning needs to feel as if it is something learners have a voice in, rather than something 'done to' them.

Malcolm Knowles (1980) makes a distinction between 'pedagogy' and on the other hand 'andragogy' (see also Chapter 1). While possibly overly simplistic and with many critics, this idea attempts to suggest a difference in the learning of younger learners (pedagogy) and the learning of adults (andragogy). The key difference between these two, for Knowles, is the 'orientation to learning' between the two groups. Within his conceptualization of andragogy, Knowles suggests that adult learners are more self-motivated and have more of a desire to engage with materials due to a desire to take ownership of and control of the direction of their own learning. Independent and project work, leading to substantial self-directed homework, is certainly a way to develop learners' self-directed orientation to learning, but only if structured and guided appropriately – as we will explore later in this chapter.

With the rise of new communication and learning technologies and the rapid spread of Web2.0 tools, we can add a third to this list. We have pedagogy and andragogy and more recently some commentators speak of 'heutagogy' (Hase and Kenyon 2007). Conceptualizations of heutagogy position the learner as 'self directed' or rather, 'self-regulated' and this is seen as almost a natural part of learning (and by implication of the human condition). The role of learning opportunities in formal settings such as schools and colleges is to allow learners to explore and develop their learning skills, and to be able to apply these learning skills with confidence. For this to take place, learners need to be able to make choices over their own learning and to work in self-directed ways. Project work and other homework can encourage the sense of independence that notions of heutagogy imply.

LINKING THEORY WITH PRACTICE

Educational theorists and writers have always tried to characterize both the nature of the learner and the nature of learning itself. Learning, perhaps surprising as so much of our professional lives is based upon engaging with it, is nonetheless a rather ambiguous notion. What is learning and what do learners bring to it? Is it something that develops inside the learner naturally or something that is stimulated from outside? Similarly, how do learners go about the process of learning, and what 'orientation' do they bring to it? In trying to unpack these points, we end up with this three-way distinction between pedagogy, andragogy and heutagogy. We might like to draw upon all three notions in our profession practice and experience. While accepting that, essentially, each is a negation of the other, we might like to try to explore times when, contradictions between theoretical ideas to one side, we embrace elements of all three. Project and assignment work certainly provide the 'space' within which we can encourage more choice, freedom and self-direction for our learners.

BEST PRACTICE – MOTIVATION AND INDEPENDENT LEARNING

There are a number of strategies you can use to develop independence and to motivate when it comes to setting longer-term project work and assignments for homework. Consider the following:

- Ask for initial proposals and have them shared with peers before work starts to take place.
- Spend considerable classroom time explaining the project – let learners see samples from previous years.
- Use the viva method to ascertain progress and to make learners feel like they have authority over their work and are 'experts' (see Chapter 7).
- Celebrate previous years' achievements – have learners come and visit and talk through their work and independent assignments.
- Have regular target-setting and monitoring meetings.
- In meetings, let learners 'set the agenda' and set their own targets as much as possible.
- Ask learners to keep a diary or log of their progress.
- Encourage learners to reflect upon the steps and decisions they are making and to have the opportunity to articulate these.
- Encourage learners to disseminate their findings with each other.
- At the end of the work, ask learners to make presentations to as diverse an audience as possible, demonstrating their work and achievements.

Table 4.1 Independent learning and support

Framework and structure *Teacher-led activities*	Teachers have the responsibility for: • Setting the time of work and final deadline • Approval of initial idea before long-term work takes place • Regular monitoring and checking • Setting regular deadlines
Independence and choice *Learner-led activities*	Learners have the responsibility for: • Thinking about and choosing approach • Format and structure of final piece (unless dictated by assessment bodies) • Logging work in journals and diaries • Research and writing up • Time management

As with most aspects of learning and teaching, the pedagogy and strategies behind developing and encouraging 'independent' learning are actually a contradictory mixture of providing a supportive framework and allowing freedom and choice at the same time (see Table 4.1).

As with all homework, the 'secret' of encouraging independent learning is support and monitoring.

Dealing with plagiarism

When asking learners to undertake research, coursework and independent project work at some point in the process you will need to engage with the issues of plagiarism and where appropriate family involvement and engagement. Use the following advice to support your reflective practice and planning on these issues.

1. Be clear with learners what plagiarism is and why it is inappropriate (see the descriptions below to help you).
2. Ensure as part of your homework policy you have a section on academic malpractice.
3. Support learners with their digital literacies and what we might call 'netracy' (see Chapters 4 and 7). If we can guide and direct learners to use the internet and any source materials correctly, then we will avoid many of the examples of 'cut and paste' that we often see.
4. If working on a formal piece of work which will be assessed by an awarding body make the awarding body's statements on malpractice clear to all learners in advice.
5. Sometimes plagiarism is a last, desperate attempt by a learner making bad choices. If you help support time management and homework patterns and practices then

you can avoid the majority of plagiarism attempts but ensure work is done according to time.

6. Following on from the point above, if you can make instructions and briefs clear and help learners to monitor their progression and set appropriate targets (see Chapter 7) then again, some aspects of malpractice can be avoided.

7. Finally – an obvious point, but a genuinely useful one to be mindful of: ensure there is actually enough time to complete the work itself. This is actually true of all homework and learning outside of the classroom. Ensure you have set realistic time frames.

We make a difference between three (often related) examples of 'academic malpractice':

Plagiarism – when learners take words not of their own and present them as their own.
Collaboration – when learners work together and swap text between work that should have been independent work.
Collusion – this is where learners enter into agreements to share confidential work or share and swap the plagiarized work of others.

LINKING THEORY TO PRACTICE

Plagiarism is in fact highly culturally specific. For some learners what we might consider to be plagiarism could be misinterpreted as 'homage' to the authority of others. Equally, some learners find it hard to develop what we refer to as critical or evaluative skills (in thinking and writing) as again to attempt to criticize the learned work of experts and authorities in their field would be seen as inappropriate. You would be wise to consider how cultural factors might impact on learning and on learners' understandings of what you require of them.

Philosophically and pedagogically the use of the term 'collaboration' is unfortunate here. We do recognize that individually assessed work *must* be individual. Yet we absolutely value the role that peer learning, conversation, peer support and dialogue play in productive and worthwhile learning experiences. However, individually assessed work is different. We, of course, are now using this word in a different context, but we feel it is an important point to make. There is a fine line here, in reality. It is absolutely appropriate to encourage students to disseminate and cascade their work, to seek help from others in the form of clarity and support. But it is not appropriate for students to present work which is not their own as their own. We actually would wish our classes to be highly 'collaborative' and wish teachers, learners and parents to collaborate together. For advice on how to engage families see the following recommendations:

TO HELP OR NOT TO HELP? THE ROLE OF PARENTS AND FAMILIES

1. Ensure parents are informed when coursework and project work starts.
2. Speak to parents about deadlines and how the timeline of the work will be patterned.
3. Communicate your expectations of how the work will be structured to both learners and their families (you might write a letter, produce a newsletter or even hold a briefing meeting).
4. Communicate what plagiarism and 'collusion' are and ask parents to be clear about the limits of their support.
5. While being clear about limits, nonetheless, encourage parental interest. Ask them to read parts of the project and to ensure they can help to monitor progress. Ask them, if appropriate with younger learners, to sign off diaries and log books each week.
6. Encourage parents to also see the value of independent work.
7. Speak to parents and learners regarding local amenities that might help the development of research skills such as local libraries, etc.
8. Try to communicate to parents the difference between encouragement/interest and support and on the other hand doing it for learners. Explain that we do need to work with parents to help learners to know what choices to make and directions to take but that they must not write parts of the work or correct it.

Research skills

Asking learners to work independently and to undertake research can be extremely rewarding, but it is also – if done properly – a huge undertaking. Its effects on learners cannot be underestimated – it can be very motivating, but if not correctly supported can lead to dissatisfaction.

BEST PRACTICE – RESEARCH SKILLS

To support research skills, think about the following strategies:

- Encourage a widespread use of all media – internet, books, newspapers, etc. Ensure that learners can manipulate all forms of text that they might need.
- Arrange sessions with libraries and maybe even your local library. Get learners familiar with the tools on offer.
- Spend time doing little 'mock' research skills practice for homework leading up to large and long-term projects. Ensure they have the tools *before* they start the work for real.
- Think about research skills in the widest possible sense: help learners not just with 'finding' and 'searching' for information from secondary sources but also making their own data through the use of questionnaires and interviews, for example.

To be able to work in a self-regulated way is a key characteristic of an independent learner. Goleman (1995) identifies 'personal intelligences' which can affect how we interact with others and take responsibility for the direction of our own learning (see also Chapter 1). For Goleman being self-directed is an 'intelligence' and something we need to practise and have support with developing. We cannot automatically expect this. This is where some teachers make a key mistake: they assume that being able to 'go off' and for homework plan their time, research something and manage their own time is easy and that older learners already have these skills. These are potentially damaging assumptions. This means that being able to develop independent working skills for any homework – not just project work – is itself an issue of differentiation (see Chapter 3). This takes us back to the idea of 'self-efficacy' as outlined earlier in this chapter. Learners need to see that they can achieve and are able to work for themselves. They will only see this with practice, support and at first, frameworks to work within. These frameworks cannot be applied *evenly* across all learners but subtly differentiated to recognize that learners' starting points for independent learning are different.

Making the most of off-site visits

We could not write a book on homework strategies and research skills without emphasizing the important role that off-site visits can have in motivating and enthusing learners of all types and ages. However rather than viewing such visits as integral to broader schemes of work (including the lessons and homework activities that precede and follow on from the visit), many learners perceive their visit as a one-off event far removed from the learning they experience back at their institution. Some off-site visits can even become the breeding ground for 'worksheet-itis', i.e. hundreds of young people wandering around exciting places of learning clutching their worksheets with dazed expressions, often lost, confused or worse still, bored and disinterested by the whole event. American writers Falk et al. (2007) argue that everyone's experience of a museum, gallery, geological site, etc. is an interactive one (see Figure. 4.1).

Whether your visit is to a museum, gallery, stately home or zoo the interactive context that teachers have to manage contains three components:

1. **the physical** (e.g. the journey to the site; its layout; objects to see/smell/touch, etc.; the noise of the place; the location of toilets and cafés; its sheer size and so on);
2. **the social** (e.g. interaction with staff and other visitors; the knowledge learners bring to the site and how this is communicated; appropriate interactions in cafés/ canteens/shops; the communication of different interests and motivations for those visiting (e.g. school pupils, families and teachers).
3. **the personal** (e.g. the frame of mind of all those visiting; their preferred learning styles; whether or not any learners have experienced or visited similar places and managing their expectations/behaviour and so on).

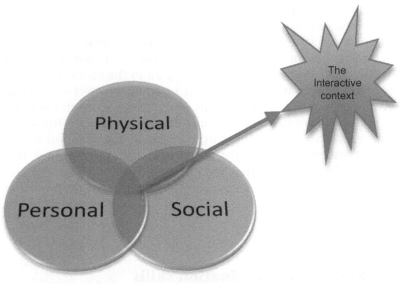

Figure 4.1   The interactive context in any off-site visit
Source: adapted from Falk et al. (2007)

On any visit the role of the teacher is to become the mediating influence for their group of learners for all three components. This means that teachers need to plan an agenda for all three areas. For example in planning the social component teachers might want to consider strategies for minimizing potential conflict between their learners and gallery staff. They may also want to consider differentiation strategies with suitable groupings of learners and so on.

BEST PRACTICE – STARTER ACTIVITIES WHEN VISITING A MUSEUM

Richard Woff from the British Museum offers two starter activities for getting learners orientated and enthused about seeing exhibits in a museum gallery:

1. Give each learner several post-its and get them on their own or in pairs to find one item made of a particular material noting down the item and the material on the post-it. They must then find another item made from a different material and so on. This is a fun five-minute activity that quickly gets learners acquainted with the particular gallery and can then be the stepping stone for more complex activities to follow.
2. Instruct learners to find five items ensuring that with each item one characteristic must be similar (e.g. both items are used for eating) and one that is completely different (e.g. both are made from completely different materials or originate from different locations). The third item will share a similarity and difference with the second and so on. As a bonus you can request that the fifth item must link back in one way to the first item on the list.

Falk et al. (2007) argue that all visits require very careful advanced planning with the management of learners' expectations (e.g. when/where they can go to shops/toilets/cafés and so on) a crucial element to planning off-site visits. This planning should be broken into three stages: pre-visit, visit and post-visit. The first stage should embrace a scheme of work for the lesson or lessons leading up to the visit composed of a sequence of activities, including homework, designed to equip learners with knowledge about why their visit is important and some of the discoveries that await them; the second will involve careful planning of the visit itself including a lesson plan with a number of activities once learners are at the site; the third part entails the lesson or lessons that follow on from the visit leading to a particular goal (e.g. a project/exhibition). It is perhaps not surprising to note that many teachers tend only to concentrate on the visit itself ignoring the importance of this three-stage process. Ensure that you have a lesson plan of activities for learners once at the site including starter activities and remember...avoid those worksheets!

Research, thinking and evaluation skills

Evaluation skills are hard to develop and cause many learners confusion. Research and evaluation are linked – in their homework and project work we require learners to not just 'find out' but to apply and interpret. Consider the following list of ways to 'do evaluation' (Kidd and Czerniawski 2010: 243–4):

- Thinking through the eyes of theories/principles/concepts;
- Using one set of theories/principles/concepts to attack another;
- Drawing attention to historical precedents to endorse/challenge; theories/principles/concepts;
- Criticising the methodology/evidence that writers use to argue their points;
- Comparing and contrasting one set of ideas with another;
- Identifying bias and or logical incoherency in ideas;
- Drawing attention to the dated nature/historical specificity of some ideas;
- Drawing attention to the ethnocentricity of some ideas;
- Pointing out the positive and negative 'contributions' of a particular idea;
- Drawing attention to the 'usefulness' (useful for whom?) of a particular idea.

Thinking about information and ideas once they have been 'found' through research is only part of the process that we require of learners. We also require them when producing homework and other work to write and express their ideas from research in an evaluative fashion. Many learners find this difficult. Use the connectives from the list below with your learners to help them develop evaluative writing skills.

CONNECTIVES FOR DEVELOPING EVALUATION

The relevance of this; This indicates; This is similar to/different from; Thus; So; Therefore; This means/does not mean; Hence; A consequence of; The implication of; The contrast between; Put simply; Illustrated by; Support for this; As shown by; This can be seen in; For example; This can be applied to; This is associated with; This leads to; This touches on; According to: The same applies to; This is confirmed by; In defence of this; A strength of this is; The value of; A benefit of; The usefulness of; An argument for; An advantage of; The importance of; This contributes to; This provides a balance to; This is significant because; This does take account of; However; Alternatively; A criticism; Another view; I disagree because; A different interpretation; On the other hand; The problem with this is; It is debatable; This is questioned; An argument against; A disadvantage of; Although; This assumes; Whereas; This cannot be explained by; This does not stand up because; This lacks support because; On the contrary; It makes little sense because; It is not true/valid because; To sum up; Having weighed up; The balance of the argument suggests; The weight of evidence suggests; The conclusion is; I agree because; returning back to the question.

Source: Kidd and Czerniawski (2010) p. 249.

Developing research, thinking and evaluation skills through homework is essential. With our changing digital landscape and mobile working practices, according to some commentators as much as 70 per cent of 'learning' in its widest understanding might be seen to be taking place outside of formal institutions such as schools, colleges and universities (Cross 2006; Dobbs 2000). By encouraging learners to undertake independent learning homework, and to develop evaluation skills, we are supporting our new generation of learners for the future.

Independent learning and e-learning tools

Many commentators suggest that the rise of the new digital landscape changes how learners relate to both knowledge and learning itself (Prensky 2001). For some, these new times present teachers, schools and colleges with a 'new learner' (and often an 'independent learner') – the *digital native*. This is someone who was born into and has grown up fully immersed in the digital world and is able to use technology and the internet in an intuitive way. The argument is that these learners need to be taught differently from previous generations (Prensky 2010). Some are critical of this idea, instead talking of an increasing 'digital divide' between those who have skills and access in and to this new digital world and those who do not (Selwyn 2009). In this new digital landscape homework and project work which require 'research skills' have consequences and implications for how learners *interact with digital sources*; how learners research and *acquire knowledge*; how new *knowledge is generated* and by whom; and what *meaning learners attach to knowledge* generated on and found within digital sources.

LINKING THEORY WITH PRACTICE

When discussing the changes taking place in education and in learning due to the rise of the global forces of communication and interactivity that the internet brings, Gonzalez (2004) refers to the rapid redundancy of knowledge as having, like atoms, an (educational) 'half-life'. Prior to the expansion of the internet, knowledge and information were harder to obtain and thus their 'currency' lasted longer. Today, as the world changes so rapidly and as the ebb and flow of global, digital information moves so quickly, the 'life' of knowledge itself diminishes. As teachers, our challenge is to help support learners to explore knowledge for themselves. In doing so when conducting homework and project work, we must support learners to be critical and evaluative of internet sources and to use technology for their own research skills. At the same time, we need to guide and support learners' critical skills. It is certainly the case that knowledge is still of prime importance in most educational systems as the object of testing and assessment, but the skills to find and then understand and 'do something with' knowledge are more important. Homework provides excellent opportunities for learners to engage with internet research and in doing so, to develop appropriate critical skills as part of their growing critical digital literacies.

In terms of research skills, it is not a case of 'out with the old, and in with the new'. Instead, Web2.0 and internet research skills need to be *added on* to existing critical and evaluative practices. In doing so, research skills need to develop as a stock of skills at hand, ready, available and working in an interconnected way as a vast repertoire for learners to draw upon. See the list of research skills below to help ensure you fully cover all skills learners might need.

EXAMPLES OF 'RESEARCH SKILLS' FOR THE DIGITAL WORLD

Learners will need to be able to:

- use catalogues to locate books and journals in libraries and find them on shelves;
- use online booking systems to locate books and to reserve materials;
- find information in books using content pages and indexes;
- use the internet to search productively for information and make appropriate choices regarding the source of the information;
- understand how to check who wrote a source and in what year;
- provide a judgment about the authenticity and authority of information found – how do we know it can be 'trusted'?
- seek out definitions of unfamiliar words and explanations of meaning of new ideas from digital and paper sources;

- identify the difference between factual knowledge and opinion and 'writing for persuasion';
- understand the difference between primary and secondary sources;
- create a basic questionnaire and set of interview questions to find out a chosen piece of information;
- collaborate and communicate with others using a variety of social media;
- make appropriate and informed choices regarding which Web2.0 tools and applications to use for specific aspects of learning, research and communication;
- produce a simple graphic to demonstrate a point supported by numerical data.

Some key research skills for our learners today are associated with what is referred to as 'digital literacy'. When we speak of 'digital literacy' we mean the skills needs to navigate, use and manipulate technological devices and tools and work appropriately in online and digital landscapes that new and emerging technology and social media have created for us. Elsewhere in this book we have used the term 'netracy' to explain this, although this would, strictly speaking, be one part of a wider digital literacy. We encourage students to work on literacy and also numeracy, but what we often do not do is to help support students with how they surf and use information from the internet. Yet, when we ask them to do coursework, research and independent work, we often expect them to do this. There is a disconnect here. Many teachers assume digital literacy in their learners or equally, some teaches are worried perhaps about their own skills in these areas. If our learners' use of the internet can be supported in homework and other project work, then it is possible to avoid examples of 'cut and paste'.

One much cited theory of learning for the 'new digital age' is the notion of 'connectivism' (Siemens 2004). To understand this idea, let us first think about another. Earlier educational theory has embraced the notion of learning as a 'constructivist' process (Vygotsky 1978) whereby learning takes place and knowledge is 'created' (or 'constructed') through learners' manipulation of and interaction with the blocks of learning: learners take new ideas and experiences and link them onto older ones, making connections in an attempt to make sense. They do this often in collaboration with others: talking, discussing and seeking to build up knowledge. Within this, as experience grows and new knowledge constructions are made, new knowledge is created. This is the rationale for many classrooms being based upon learner talk and learner activity and interactivity with others. For *connectivism* (Siemens 2004) knowledge and learning are a product of interaction of the group: of the connections and building networks between learners. As technology enables new means by which we communicate and interact, this theory suggests that knowledge is not internal to the meaning-making processes of the individual but rather, a product of the networked-self.

New and emerging technologies provide many opportunities. They can:

- support learners in accessing easily information;
- help learners to work in non-traditional places and settings in a more 'mobile' fashion (see Chapter 7);

- provide opportunities to connect to and interact with others over vast differences of time and space;
- provide the means through which, with careful use of homework, classrooms can be 'flipped' and learning and curriculum content be 'delivered' outside of class and skills development and independent learning take place inside lessons where the teacher is present.

> **FREQUENTLY ASKED QUESTIONS – HOW CAN I MOST SUCCESSFULLY USE TECHNOLOGY FOR RESEARCH AND INDEPENDENT LEARNING?**
>
> Think about incorporating the following into your regular practice:
>
> 1. Encourage learners to use forums or blogs set up by you to share experiences of research and useful links and tips.
> 2. Support learners to develop social bookmarking practices where they can share links and recommended sources of information (see Chapter 7).
> 3. Support learners to set up their own blog and use it as an online diary or journal to record and evidence their progress in their work.
> 4. Explore with learners how they might use key internet sites that you have authenticated – take them through the sites and show how they can be useful.
> 5. Use synchronous (in real time) discussion and chat rooms on a regular basis at a pre-arranged time so that even 'at a distance' learners can work together and receive support.
> 6. Encourage mobile working, using Wi-Fi, hot spots and local amenities to be able to develop work patterns and practices that fit into their lives.

Technology and technological devices and internet-based tools are not just mediums through which learners can do homework, but they are places within which independent research can be carried out and also places within which virtual classrooms can exist.

Conclusion

In this chapter we argue that research skills and homework are inter-linked with independent learning, thinking skills, evaluation, 'personal intelligences' and digital literacy. The learning 'rewards' for setting projects and long-term assignments are huge – the skills they develop will truly empower learners to become lifelong learners. But just as the rewards are large, the efforts required to support and set up are great. Think carefully about how you will structure large assignments and homework and what role technological, thinking and evaluation skills will play in this.

QUESTIONS FOR PROFESSIONAL DEVELOPMENT

1. How might you incorporate support of learners' digital literacy into your general support of their study skills? This is crucial in the changing world we live in.
2. Think about how you set up independent work: what structures will you put in place and how will you help learners to monitor their own progression? These issues of structures, choices and monitoring are absolutely essential in ensuring all learners can develop appropriate independent learning skills no matter what their starting point.
3. What research skills do your learners need to develop? Think about a skills audit with them as a place to start before you commence longer-term or larger-scale project work for homework.
4. How can learners log and record their progress through learning outside of the classroom? Does new technology play a role in supporting learners to do this?

5   Assessing homework

Introduction – trust your instincts

As a topic of research, assessment is not new, however since the mid-2000s a renewed focus on different ways to assess for learning has emerged since the work of Black and William's (1998) *Inside the Black Box* and the Assessment Reform Group (2002). Their conclusions are significant for all teachers considering homework as a strategy for learning and underpin our belief that homework, as a significant form of assessment, should be homework for learning (HfL). The word 'assessment' for many potential teachers conjures up images of exams, essays and a stack of homework to mark. In fact good assessment of homework, when correctly and skilfully carried out, can motivate and inspire learners to perform beyond their own expectations in all formal learning scenarios. It can also be life changing.

Trust your professional instincts when your own assessment strategies and records highlight discrepancies in records passed onto you by previous colleagues/institutions (for example, many cases of dyslexia are first spotted by vigilant colleagues marking homework in sixth form centres and FE colleges despite those learners having attended primary and secondary schools and the disability going unnoticed). After introducing you to essential concepts associated with assessment this chapter offers ideas to support you in the organization, facilitation and assessment of strategies for learning outside the classroom.

What is assessment?

A lot of the work that teachers do is to provide opportunities for assessment *of* learning. In other words strategies that:

- summarize what has been learnt at a given point in time;
- tell teachers where learners are (without necessarily identifying the source of difficulty or how to improve);
- provide outcomes to be used to celebrate achievement and success for learners and schools: ways of doing this include displays, presentations, merits and through nationally accredited award schemes.

When planning strategies for learning outside of the classroom it helps to think of four broad strategies of assessment. First *initial* or *diagnostic* assessment refers to tasks that occur at the start of any course/unit/module designed to measure if the course the learner is on is best suited to it. Typically it looks at the sorts of support a learner might require (e.g. literacy, numeracy, etc.). Second, *summative* assessment refers to 'snapshots' taken at any one time, of a learner's progress (e.g. public examinations, end of term tests, etc.). While this provides vital information for both learner and teacher most summative assessments offer little or no information to inform the future progress of the learner. Third, *formative* assessment is any type of assessment that informs that future progress. It is often ongoing and can be informally carried out (e.g. a corridor chat with a student to offer advice on the next assignment) or formally carried out (e.g. written feedback with targets at the end of a piece of homework). Finally *ipsative* assessment refers to the process of learner self-assessment, that is the learner identifies their own progress and identifies their own needs. It also is a form of assessment that recognizes the progress (or 'distance travelled') made by the individual regardless of any external benchmarks.

> **BEST PRACTICE - BE S.M.A.R.T. WHEN SETTING HOMEWORK TASKS**
>
> Remember that all your homework instructions and feedback should be:
>
> - specific, i.e. refer exactly to what students should do rather than issuing instructions or praise that is generalized, vague and unclear;
> - measurable, i.e. any activity should have an outcome that the teacher can identify (e.g. one speech, one photograph, one whole paragraph of writing, etc.);
> - achievable, i.e. the task should challenge the learner but not be something they cannot achieve. It can be incredibly demotivating to set out on a piece of work and realize you cannot achieve its outcome;
> - realistic, i.e. it must be something the learner can do (for example, if a learner does not posses a television it will be impossible for them to do an analysis of TV advertisements);
> - timed, i.e. assessment tasks need to be set within a time limit (e.g. 'you have ten minutes to . . .' or 'this homework must be handed in by 2.00 pm on Friday', etc.).

Assessment *for* Learning (AfL)

Black and William (1998) argue that while regular formative assessment is extremely effective in raising academic standards, assessment practices in general have often been little understood by the teaching profession. There is, for example, little evidence to suggest that AfL techniques have been widely embraced by teachers as part of their homework strategies. This is one reason why we emphasize Homework *for* Learning (HfL) as an underpinning philosophy of this book.

FREQUENTLY ASKED QUESTIONS – WHAT IS 'ASSESSMENT *FOR* LEARNING'?

Recognizing the negative effects that some sorts of assessment activities create, Black and William (1998) draw a distinction between assessment *of* and *for* learning stating that 'Assessment for learning is any assessment for which the first priority in its design and practice is to serve the purpose of promoting pupils' learning' (Black and Wiliam 1998: 18). AfL occurs at all stages of the learning process with learners knowing at the start of any course what they are expected to learn. Through *initial/diagnostic assessment* the teacher and learner work together to understand what she or he already knows about the topic as well as to identify any gaps or misconceptions. Through the use of *formative assessment* the teacher and student assess collaboratively the learner's knowledge, what she or he needs to learn to improve and extend this knowledge, and how the learner can best get to that point.

Evidence from the Assessment Reform Group has shown that how assessment of learning is reported back to the learner (feedback) affects their motivation to learn. This body of work has led to renewed attention on the adoption of so-called 'medal and mission' assessment strategies. The 'medal' relates to any positive aspects of the work being assessed and the 'mission' draws attention to the learner on targets for future learning. This 'formative' emphasis on the nature and purpose of assessment prioritizes 'feedforward' over and above 'feedback' suggesting that better school/college results will follow from better learning and by developing and maintaining pupils' motivation to learn rather than an overemphasis on the often demotivating effects of summative testing. With AfL's emphasis on pupil autonomy and the encouragement of pupils to work independently there is an obvious synergy between AfL and homework strategies. It is therefore worth considering the following recommended principals of the Assessment Reform Group when considering the sorts of tasks you might be setting. These principals are:

- Actively involve learners in their own assessment.
- Involve the sharing of learning objectives with learners.

- Help learners know and recognize what they are aiming for.
- Combine the use of effective questioning techniques before or after initiation of any assessment activity.
- Involve both teacher and learner in the reviewing and reflecting on the collected assessment information.
- Provide feedback, which leads to learners recognizing their next steps in their learning and how to take them.
- Promote confidence so that everyone can improve.

LINKING THEORY WITH PRACTICE

When evaluating different homework strategies draw on the ideas of Black and William (1998) and the Assessment Reform Group (2002) and reflect on the following criteria when assessing how effective your homework strategy might be:

1. Is it valid, i.e. does it assess what it is supposed to?
2. Is it reliable, i.e. can the assessment and its judgment be repeated by another teacher or with another group under the same conditions with similar results?
3. Is it adequate/sufficient, i.e. is the data sufficient to tell you what you need to know about the group, the learner and your teaching strategies?
4. Is it fair, i.e. can all learners engage with the tasks and is support available to those that cannot?
5. Is it appropriate, i.e. does it develop skills needed for the particular programme of study?
6. Is it authentic, i.e. is the work being assessed the work of the learner submitting it?
7. Is it transparent, i.e. do all those being assessed understand what they are being asked to do and why?

To grade or not to grade?

Institutional policies vary but in general if marking provides a grade and an annotation learners are more likely to pay attention to one and not the other, i.e. either the grade or the annotation, so choose carefully which technique you will use and vary this but be consistent in how/when you vary making sure that you deploy both strategies over a period of time. Providing the particular learner is happy with this, photocopy any graded work that is very good and either display it on the wall or disseminate it to students to model the good practice of exemplary work carried out by their peers. When annotating focus on how the student can improve their work to the next level. Remember to set SMART targets (see above) on any written feedback ensuring that the learner is capable of carrying out the target you set.

While practice and academia vary enormously on the merits of how feedback should be written, try to avoid the use of red pen when commenting on students' work. Many EAL and SEN students associate the colour red with being wrong and its use can demotivate many learners. Many excellent teachers consequently use green pen when marking work. Avoid crosses for the same reasons and underline weaknesses, adding comments where necessary on how the learner can improve. By all means tick but ensure that you do not just tick for the sake of it – underline the work/sentence that the tick refers to so that the learner can quickly identify what it is they are doing well.

Strategies to manage marking

You cannot mark every piece of homework rigorously. However your ability to maintain consistently excellent teaching and assessment of homework will, in part, depend on the strategies you develop to deal with the high volume of marking that is an inevitable aspect of teaching. It is therefore important that you reflect on your own organizational skills when marking work. With the sophistication of computer programmes and computer-based assessment tracking, there are a variety of ways in which you can record your assessment decisions (we are still huge fans of the old paper based record keeping for those quick 30 second corridor discussions with colleagues). Either way the administrative burden of teaching is huge and while we certainly do not advocate short cuts in terms of assessment, finding a variety of ways to cope with marking and record keeping is prudent and will help you maintain longevity in the profession backed up by the energy, enthusiasm and creativity required to motivate your learners. The following strategies are suggestions to help ease your organization and marking:

- When you collect work instruct your learners to keep their exercise books open at the page you will be marking to save time later trying to find the correct piece of work to mark.
- When giving written feedback focus on five learners in every lesson to which you give in-depth comments and limit the feedback for the rest of the class. Ensure that you rotate this so that every four to five taught sessions *all* learners will have received the quality formative feedback you deem necessary.
- It takes five times longer to write something down than to say it. Many learners appreciate verbal feedback more than written commentary so ensure that you work in opportunities to provide individually feedback on homework. For example, this can also be done on a rota verbally feeding back to five students in every lesson.
- Create templates/exemplars/guidelines that learners working in pairs can use to peer mark their work ensuring that after they have completed peer assessment you didactically explain/clarify any emerging issues that learners need to understand.

- Colour code batches of folders/exercise books in any one class. For example, put a red sticker on one quarter of the books, a green sticker on the next, etc. This means that you can then call in those learners' work with red sticker one week, a blue sticker the next, etc. and spread the mark load while ensuring that everything is covered.
- Develop a system of codes in both your mark book and the feedback you give your students. Code your target setting so that students know exactly which areas they must improve on (e.g. 'P' = presentation; 'D' = more detail; 'E' = evidence; 'K' = key concepts; 'SPAG' = spelling and grammar, etc.). Using your records, you can then ensure that any targets set build on those that you have set previously rather than simply setting the same targets again and again to the same student. Many teachers use 'WWW' (what 'went well') and 'EBI' ('even better if') in their feedback. Traffic Lights (Green for excellent, Amber for satisfactory/partially understood and Red for unsatisfactory/not understood) can be used in a variety of ways as codes for you to record how well students are doing.
- Similarly devise a set of codes (e.g. Sp = Spelling; C = concept, etc.) and write these codes as a form of feedback to your learners. Learners must examine their written work and correctly identify what the codes mean and verbally feedback to you their corrections in light of the codes you have written (e.g. how to spell that word; their correct interpretation of the concept, etc.). Individual tasks can always be set in the written feedback and time allocated in any lesson for the work to be reviewed and comments to be followed up (e.g. 'ask your partner to explain X to you...'; 'go to page 57 and read and then explain this to....', etc.).
- Invent a coding or short-hand system in the homework sections of your records e.g. colour code homework with Red (not done); Orange (unfinished); Pink (work not in book); Blue (book/work not seen).
- Get out that diary and stagger when you set homework for different classes marking each batch of work the moment it comes in. Do this regularly so that learners can see that you are on the ball with who has, and who has not done their work for you.

Be selective about what you mark, when and why and do not mark unnecessarily. Timetable your marking choosing a time of day and location where there are no distractions (remember that types of marking vary as do suitable locations, for example many teachers mark work on train/bus journeys, etc.). Time spent on work should be appropriate to the work done so remember that the first three to four pieces of work you mark will always take longer than the rest. Make sure that you choose three to four students across the ability range to mark first so that you get a good overall sense of what the standard of work will be. Do not mark out every single mistake but rather focus on specific issues related to any generic targets you will be setting for the class at the end of the assessed piece of work. Finally involve parents/guardians in the homework process, telephoning them or emailing them when things go well as well as badly. Explain homework policies to them (e.g. at parents evenings) and get them to sign homework planners as and when you see fit.

BEST PRACTICE – ON-LINE TESTING

Many subjects use on-line testing as a way in which homework can be set which requires little or no marking on the part of the teacher. While we do not advocate 'little or no marking', a range of assessment strategies is vital and can ease the workload of both teacher and student if carefully managed. Increasingly in many institutions students are issued with a password and will then sit a vocabulary/concept test based on the work that they have covered with the teacher. Learners that do not reach the required pass mark must re-sit the text at the end of the school/college day. Providing the website is appropriate students tend to revise and pass not wishing to re-sit the test at the end of the day. Increasingly most website-based tests are fun and students enjoy this form of assessment.

Easing that workload – strategies requiring minimal written feedback

Balancing the often-conflicting institutional demands that teachers experience with their desire to do the best possible job they can in developing the knowledge, understanding and enthusiasm of their learners is a hard trick to pull off. In recognition of this dilemma we offer, in this section, some strategies to complement those elsewhere in this book that can be slotted into your wider repertoire of homework activities rather than become a substitute for them.

Set tasks for your learners to do the following:

- Update the class on news headlines during that week. They can bring in articles on any theme you choose. A nice touch is to request occasionally that they must be able to take questions on the topic from their peers.
- Create a quiz/test/wordsearch/crossword/puzzle/photo montage that learners can swap and answer with another member of the class before they assess how they have performed. Make sure that they bring with them the correct answers.
- Create spider diagrams, flow charts or any sort of diagrammatic representation of key themes related to what they study ensuring that the best of these are displayed.
- Watch a particular play/film/news/documentary and then compile questions to test others in class in the next lesson.
- Summarize/review an article/chapter/report/review/picture ensuring that the summary is brought to your lesson attached to the item that has been summarized. Your learners will have highlighted key concepts on the actual item and they can refer to the line number/page (if appropriate) to indicate examples of where these appear in the text. You can, in addition, ask pupils in pairs to explain these concepts.
- Choreograph/direct and perform a dance, mime or scene that relates to a key theme/concept/incident of significance to their studies.

- Design leaflets/banners/posters/flags/flyers/mindmaps on a topic of your choice justifying the choice of design to a partner/group member.
- Using any items from home create a model that relates to the topic you are teaching. You can embellish this by stipulating the sorts of materials and or items learners can use (e.g. if the theme is the environment then get learners to create a model of a recycling plant using recyclable packaging from food containers, cleaning materials, etc.).
- Bring in music that relates to a particular theme and get learners to write down any key terminology that appears in the song.
- Carry out an interview on a topic of your choice with somebody in the immediate community and either audio or video record this to be played back to the whole class.
- Have pictures taken of them on their mobile phone or any other device as a way of proving that they have indeed carried out the task (e.g. creating an exam revision timetable; interviewing a family member).
- Take photos on a particular theme in a museum or exhibition that you specify (ensuring that this is allowed within the institution concerned) and get learners to present and explain the significance of their chosen three photos.
- Create a story board of an event or process which is then explained to the class.
- Create a display of a key person drawing lines to visual representations of the work they are associated with. This can be done traditionally with magazine cut outs, etc. but can also be done deploying one of the many programmes available (e.g. SpiderScribe).
- Create a revision schedule to be displayed on a wall at home and provide a photo of this brought into the class to be shared with partners discussing best practice.
- Draw a caricature of a key person/character/stereotype justifying why certain characteristics are associated with the caricature.
- Prepare for their exams by bringing in folders, exercise books, etc. In addition to other resources, homework can be assembled thematically or chronologically throughout the year. Create a pro-forma that has all the essential ingredients you would expect in an ideal folder and get learners to peer assess each other's collected work.
- Produce a plan for an essay to be done in class which can then be peer marked (seek out model answers for this to give to peers after the essay is completed).
- Ask learners to film (using their mobile phone or devices made available to them) any activity you require (e.g. carrying out interviews/questionnaires) and randomly choose a sample of learners to show their films to the class.

The emphasis in these tasks is on the value of learner talk and your ability to listen, watch and motivate your learners. You *will* need to offer feedback but with careful walking around the class, checking and ticking where and when necessary you can, and indeed *must* verbally feedback to the class. However this can be done as a broad summary of the work you assess flagging up the strengths and weaknesses of what you have seen.

Conclusion

As ex-teachers we recognize that your workload is enormous. In addition to teaching the reality for most teachers is one dominated by meetings with parents, subject departments, school/college governors and other outside agencies all backed up with statutory and institutional paperwork and, oh yes, there is that marking to do. While we emphasize the importance of clear, targeted written feedback we also recognize the need for dynamic, energetic and enthusiastic teachers who do not risk premature 'burn out'. We also recognize that getting learners to self-assess and your role in appropriately supporting this process is essential for their learning.

QUESTIONS FOR PROFESSIONAL DEVELOPMENT

1. What is your philosophy of assessment? Where do you see HfL positioned within that philosophy? The categories that you develop within your assessment records speak volumes about the sort of teacher you are and the assessment strategies you consider important. Try to develop your own thoughts about what is important or not when assessing the needs of your learners and recognize that there is more to assessment than just measuring the academic output of learners. What might be the implications of this in terms of the sorts of homework strategies you set, when and why?
2. Many teachers adopt peer and/or self-assessment strategies when marking homework. To what extent do you think this is appropriate and what other forms of 'learner voice' could you introduce into the assessment of homework that could inform the progress of learners?
3. In what ways is the data compiled about your students used by you to assess your performance as their teacher? To what extent do you believe that such data is useful in serving this purpose?
4. Predicted grades (what a teacher thinks a learner will get from a test/ examination), aspirational grades (what a learner is working towards) and minimum target grades (norm referenced against the rest of the national cohort) are commonly used in schools and colleges. What criticisms can you identify in their usage? How can you adapt your practice in relation to homework, to ensure that such criticism is not warranted?

6   Supporting learners

Introduction – assumptions and cultures

The setting of homework is by no means simple – it is a highly complex act. Yet teachers often take a lot for granted when we think about and set homework. Common assumptions about homework and homework cultures include the following:

- Learners see the point of doing homework.
- Learners have an appropriate space at home in which to work.
- Learners have appropriate 'quiet time' in which to work.
- Learners have a family ethos which supports and values homework.
- Parents and family members will provide the right support and will help monitor homework practices (without intervening too much or inappropriately).
- Learners have access to the equipment they need.
- Learners have internet access.

Assumptions that homework is unproblematic and that everyone understands the point of homework and is able to complete it fail to understand the diverse realities of the lives of the learners we teach: the physical and social conditions under which homework practices are conducted can vary considerably. This makes homework (along with all aspects of education and educational routines and interactional encounters) an example of what sociologists call a 'social practice' (Bourdieu 1977 and 1990). Social practices are routines, heavily culturally specific and imbued with habitual (everyday) patterns that are framed by social forces. Social practices are a product of the interplay between the structures of society, organizational routines and the everyday actions of 'ordinary' people. For example, while the same learners might be doing the 'same' homework, since the learners themselves are different and their social circumstances will be different, the meaning of the homework practices themselves will be different. This is not to operate with a deficit model of some learners from lower socio-economic backgrounds, nor to assume that middle class parents will always be 'interested' in homework completion. Rather, it is to point out that if we set homework (and we should) we should also begin to try to understand the social situations, forces and circumstances that shape and affect how it is completed.

LINKING THEORY WITH PRACTICE

The French sociologist Bourdieu (1977 and 1990) uses the term social capital to refer to behaviours and social qualities that are 'held' by some groups and valued by society and its culture as a whole. Valuing homework and providing the means for children to achieve successful outcomes is itself an example of social capital. Whereas some parents might not engage, others will. Some parents will see the value of homework while others might be more dismissive. This will affect how homework is perceived at home and even the opportunities home-life might provide for the successful completion of homework or otherwise.

In this chapter we make a distinction between homework *practices* and homework *cultures*. When we talk about homework practices we think about how learners go about the process of preparing, organizing and carrying out homework tasks. This includes the location the work is done in, the time it takes, if there are regular routines in place and the physical environment and tools at hand. When we talk of homework cultures, we refer to how schools and colleges as organizations and learning communities establish the value and significance of homework amongst staff, learners and parents.

Establishing and leading homework cultures

The following checklist builds on previous chapters of this book and provides ideas for ways in which successful homework cultures and the policies that guide them can be embedded within all learning institutions:

- Make sure that homework policies are clear to all staff so that teachers can accommodate departmental wishes in the composition of homework timetables.

- Ensure that the guardians/parents of your learners have copies of the homework policy of your institution and, if possible, a homework plan for the year/term/semester.
- Consult learners about what they believe to be the most useful homework activities and ensure that their views are taken into account when devising homework policies.
- Support all teachers with persistent homework defaulters utilizing the referral system within your institution. Ensure that learners are aware of this system and build on their awareness when monitoring homework completion rates.
- Ensure that all teachers set homework that is valuable, ensuring that there is progression and relevance and that these activities are in line with departmental policies.
- Make sure that all learners are aware of the reason that homework is set, the methods used to mark and assess it and the benefits gained from successfully completing it.
- When creating departmental schemes of work ensure that homework activities take into consideration the recommended amount of time young people should spend on homework activities (see Chapter 1).
- Remember that not all learners come equipped with good organizational skills. Ensure that all learners have the ability and opportunity to take down the instructions and deadlines for all homework activities.
- Where appropriate give learners an ideal/recommended/target time for the assignment/activity/project giving them the flexibility to decide how and when they should work on these tasks (ensuring that these target times fit within institutional deadlines).
- Provide learners with their own student journals/diaries (or instruct learners to create their own). Learners should ensure that they write down the instructions, date and deadline of the task set plus any resources they may need. Where appropriate, once the task is completed a parent or guardian should sign off this activity and the learner should note how long they have spent on the task as a means of monitoring and improving their personal time management.
- Make sure that all learners keep their journals/diaries with them at all times.
- Where and when appropriate use these documents to write comments of praise as well as any disciplinary measures, ensuring that that these documents are consistently built into all systems and policies within the institution.
- Where and whenever possible distribute homework timetables at the start of each academic year, term and/or semester to each learner and their guardian/parent.
- Communicate directly with parents/guardians of persistent homework defaulters when complaints regarding the same learner have been passed on by via another member of staff.
- Where appropriate all form tutors should sign and monitor homework journals/diaries for any irregularities in homework completion rates and parental signatures (where appropriate) ensuring that persistent defaulters are referred up through the correct institutional channels.
- Form tutors should rigorously follow up on any concerns expressed to them by other members of the teaching staff in regards to non-completion of homework activities on their behalf.
- Depending on the nature and purpose of the learning institution create group league tables for homework completion and display these in each workshop,

classroom or studio and consider appropriate prizes (e.g. best grade, best presentation, best effort).

- Regularly display fresh examples of work completed by students and ensure that these examples are pointed out to learners when introducing a new task.
- Provide homework 'clubs' or learning spaces appropriately staffed for those learners who may not have suitable conditions at home to successfully complete the tasks they are set.

Don't forget working in this way is not your individual responsibility but something to share with all colleagues. Ensure that all support staff are empowered to work with teaching staff in the creation and facilitation of homework strategies and the resources that accompany them. Where possible forward schemes of work so that these important members of staff can prepare additional resources and prepare themselves for any 'bottlenecks' that may emerge during the course of the academic year.

Institutional responses to homework

Homework is not just a question of the choices individual teachers make. Nor is its outcome the sole result of the work individual learners do. Rather, what homework comes to 'mean' in any given class, is the result of the interaction between:

- classroom teaching
- teacher and learner emotional intelligence (see Chapters 1 and 4)
- school policies
- leadership styles and structures
- monitoring processes
- individual motivation
- resource provision
- time and spatial factors.

In this way we begin to understand schools and colleges as complex social systems in their own right. This means that homework cultures are the result of school leadership and management and the responsibility of everyone to both establish and maintain. Homework policies and homework support opportunities are something to be planned, discussed, monitored and invested in.

Location, location, location – creating the perfect work environment

Location is vital for homework – as it is for all learning environments, both inside and outside of the classroom. When we think of the suitability of the location, we might at first think about the home environment, and immediately conclude that we have no means by which to affect this. This is wrong on two counts. First, we need to think about *all* possible 'homework' environments – your institutional library, the local library, home, classrooms at lunchtime, after-school clubs and even virtual and digital spaces. Second, while we cannot have a direct effect over the logistics and location of home working environments we can communicate recommendations to both learners and to their families. We need to both guide and support learners to understand the point of homework, and also the more effective homework practices.

Try some of the following ideas:

- Arrange a visit to your local library guided by a librarian who can show learners the resources and facilities. Get them enrolled if they are not already.
- Encourage your school or college librarian to do the same – a tour and a support session with how to use the library is essential, especially if it has specialist equipment, audio books, PCs, etc.
- Write a newsletter home to parents explaining the value of homework. Include with this some tips and pointers for setting up 'homework-friendly' spaces at home. Take some of the ideas from this book to help you.
- Get older learners to visit your class and act as 'homework role models' explaining both how they organize homework and where they work and why. Get them to go through the advantages and disadvantages of different spaces including local amenities you may not know about.
- Get learners to do a 'homework quiz' where you ask them questions about good and less good homework practices and locations. Maybe learners could rank different locations and set-ups based upon the homework activity (remember – different places will lead themselves to different ways of working and also different types of tasks).
- Create a 'homework engaged' or 'homework ready' award. Learners would need to build up points by visiting locations such as local libraries, galleries, museums, internet cafes and so on to demonstrate their effective homework routines.
- Offer to sponsor local amenities with a 'supporting learning' award if they are engaged in practices that help support the homework of local children and young adults.
- Create an 'Are you homework ready?' campaign poster – maybe run a competition for the best design. Put the poster up around walls and noticeboards with homework hints and tips for planning, preparing and also setting up working spaces.
- Run a series of focus groups with learners across your whole institution. Get them to identify what practices and locations work for them and why. Collate this data and disseminate through the Virtual Learning Environment (VLE), tutorials, newsletters, assemblies, etc. In particular, explore with new entrants into your school and college what (1) homework was like in their last school, and (2) what their expectations of homework are now. As we have said elsewhere (see Chapter 1), as a profession we know relatively little about younger learners' perceptions of homework (see Hallam 2005; Warton 2001) and this would be a great contribution to your own local understandings.

- Finally, write up all the best advice you can gather from your own learners (this gives it a really localized and personal stamp) and put together some VLE pages for the school or college. Engage other colleagues to help you to do this. Make homework a collective focus of all your endeavours.

Above all (as with all learning and learning how to learn) encourage critical reflection in your own learners. Get them to articulate how they prepare and plan to work and how they set up their working space and environment. Be sensitive to the fact that some learners might not be allowed to visit local amenities on their own, or that some learners do not have individual bedrooms or perhaps a family PC. Factor this into individual conversations if you can, with appropriate confidentiality. Get them to identify their barriers to homework completion that are *physical, equipment* and *time*. Then help them to find and think about solutions. These are essential conversations and vital for building homework and wider learning cultures.

We sometimes refer to schools and colleges as 'communities of practice' (Wenger 1998), meaning that they are places where colleagues learn from each other through discussion and collaboration and through sharing approaches to the work practices they have in common, seeking to develop common approaches and cultures. Homework is as much an issue of institutional culture and ethos as it is individual motivation and ability.

LINKING THEORY WITH PRACTICE

The notion of a community of practice comes from Wenger (1998) who looks at how professionals learn while in places of employment and how new entrants into professions become socialized and learn to fit into new groups and organizations. Communities of practice develop shared understandings through common experiences. When establishing common approaches to any aspect of learning and teaching in a school or college (homework, behaviour, attendance, etc.) the community of practitioners need to establish a common cultural ground. If homework practices vary considerably, and with little professional dialogue and discussion, then it is likely that standards will vary too. Communities of teachers and learners taking homework as an issue of mutual conversation and planning will considerably improve the development of homework cultures.

How homework 'works' is a matter of negotiation and communication between teaching staff, subject teams, faculties and pastoral staff. For example, setting regular homework in relation to school and college policies requires agreement over the policy – both its aims and what it looks like in practice. Equally, running homework support and homework clubs are opportunities for staff to collaborate and share both experience and also the burden of time.

Homework clubs and institutional support

Establishing homework clubs is part of wider process of developing homework cultures. For successful homework cultures to develop a number of key factors need to be in place:

- homework policies that are targeted across cohorts and year groups which determine how often work is set and assessed;
- regular routines and structures for both learners and teachers;
- dedicated physical space before and after lesson time for learners to work;
- additional staff time to support individuals and groups – which can be both self directed and also referred;
- resources available to ensure homework can be completed – books, PCs;
- effective and meaningful assessment of homework;
- clear linkage of homework to the curriculum and to wider formal assessment and learning outcomes;
- monitoring and tracking of homework completion;
- engagement and communication with families;
- support for learners to plan and organize study skills effectively;
- cultures of learning that encourage peer support.

Homework clubs can be organized in a variety of ways from the very informal to formal, as Table 6.1 indicates. Homework clubs can be combined with other ventures such as breakfast clubs or family learning workshops where parents and children work together collaboratively. For example, there is a rich tradition across many urban multi-cultural areas for members of some ethnic communities to develop what are often called 'Saturday Schools'. These are, in the main, community volunteers working in community centres

Table 6.1 Homework clubs – types and differences

Informal	Individual teachers can make themselves available over lunch hours or at other times
	Teachers should encourage groups of peers to work together to complete tasks outside of lesson time using school or college resources and spaces
	Teachers and support staff can support learners to sit in quiet rooms if they need to continue to work
Formal	Institutions should encourage faculties and subject teams to hold regular 'surgery' hours for older learners on a drop in basis
	Faculties, subject teams and learning support staff run formal workshops which learners can either be referred to by other staff or can self-refer
	Formal cohort-specific clubs can be set up that learners and their families need to sign up for
	Peer mentoring and buddying schemes should be developed with staff organization and monitoring

and other such places (church halls, libraries, etc.), supporting local children with their learning, classwork and homework outside of formal school time. Some urban schools have noticed the development of these traditions and have responded by inviting families into the school to support homework clubs and to even learn alongside children where applicable (these joint lessons are often based around ESOL support). In all these examples, clubs become part of the regular structures of support and regular routines of the cultural life of the school or college community. The reason why these community practices are successful is because there is a great deal of enthusiasm and there are well-motivated people willing to take the time necessary to develop a culture of participation. In schools and colleges, for clubs to be established and to be successful and for homework cultures to 'take off' and have a sustainable life of their own, teachers need to have high expectations of learners. But high expectations can only be met if the infrastructure is there and the personal and emotional encouragement supports learners joining, taking part, attending and feeling that they are getting back something of value.

FREQUENTLY ASKED QUESTIONS – HOW CAN I SET UP A HOMEWORK CLUB FOR MY LEARNERS?

Think about both the need and the demand for a homework club. What group would you start the club with and why? Which class/year group has the most need, but on the other hand, where might be the potential demand and initial enthusiasm? You would be best advised, right from the very start, to speak to older learners and other staff and try to create a club based upon the collective efforts of all these people – a true 'community of practice'. Involving other learners in these practices is a very transparent action, and such transparency and 'ownership' would directly benefit and support learners' self-confidence, motivation, community involvement and leadership skills. If your institution has a staff-student council you might like to seek their advice. Alternatively, there might be small sources of income to fund some costs. You will never know if you don't ask!

If you were interested in setting up a homework club or support activity you might find other professional benefits and avenues to explore developing out from it. For example, it might mean you are able to run support sessions for colleagues to help them to develop homework and homework club ideas of their own. You could work with other schools (perhaps your feeder schools) to support them in setting up similar activities. You might see this as contributing to a piece of action research (see Chapter 8). You could use the 'student voice' (the capturing of student opinions and views) as a means to evaluate the successfulness of the homework support provision (see Chapter 8). Ensure that the provision you put in place can be continued over a regular period of time and is not just a piecemeal or reactive solution to homework. When thinking about supporting learners with homework, support needs to be both sustainable and also scalable. By sustainable we mean that the practice and activity you set up will exist and continue to exist over time (maybe even without you, if, for example you moved job or changed role). By scalable we mean that the activity, if popular and successful can be added on to and developed more, and as the need for it and the demand grows, this demand can still be met.

If you do establish homework clubs and other structures for support you are best advised to evaluate them – you will be required at some point to justify time spent on new activities and as a professional you are also expected to be engaged in reflective practice. In his book *Becoming a Critically Reflective Teacher* Brookfield (1995) identifies a very useful structure for critical reflective practice for teachers that would apply to our example of a homework club here. Brookfield suggests that we adopt four 'lenses' through which we can think about our practices and their effects and consequences:

1. autobiographical – our own reflections;
2. students – using and engaging with the student voice;
3. colleagues – working with and seeking the critical opinions of those you work with and directly alongside;
4. literature – what research says about the practice you are engaged with.

In using these four 'lenses' you would be able to think in a more informed away about the successfulness of homework support strategies. As we have said elsewhere in this chapter, this might be the start of some very interesting action research as you start to establish new routines and support and guidance structures for homework practices and support policies and mechanisms (see Chapter 2 for a further discussion).

Time management and planning

We can identify five key barriers to homework completion.

1. Difficulty of work – is the work too hard?
2. Misunderstanding tasks – are instructions too complex to unpack?
3. Motivation – will learners lack motivation as they see the work as too hard to do?
4. Space – is there a lack of private and adequate space within your institution or at home?
5. Place – are there difficulties of location and environment?
6. Time – is there enough time or does family life impact upon potential available time?
7. Resources – are learners lacking adequate tools and equipment?

Barriers to homework completion are complex. Some might rest with learners and some with home environments but others can be solved through changes in your own teaching strategies. For example, some learners may not see the point as homework itself is not marked or does not connect to the curriculum and to classwork in an obvious way (see Chapter 2 for a fuller discussion). Think about how you might set up the homework task and make it clear with correctly communicated instructions. Plan for homework so that it can be completed with varying resources and equipment and in a number of different locations. Think very carefully about the time a homework task takes to complete and ensure your deadlines are realistic. Think about what other homework learners have. 'Time' as a barrier has a very complex nature. It is both something fixed and 'beyond our control' (and often feels like this), and yet we can begin to plan and map out what time we do have and take control of work habits and patterns. We need to encourage learners to have control and ownership over their homework routines.

Support with homework routines

There are a variety of ways that learners can be guided and supported with homework (and other independent working and 'study' habits), as indicated below. We often help support younger learners with homework timetables and planners and diaries, but sometimes neglect the older learners. It is sometimes taken for granted, for example, that older learners know how to organize their homework patterns, but this is not necessarily the case.

- Some schools and colleges provide planners and diaries or logs for learners to use to record homework.
- Use of the VLE could be made to record all homework tasks. You could provide additional content such as videos or audio podcasts explaining the tasks in more detail.
- Your organization could set up a 'text message' (SMS) alert to remind learners of deadlines and tasks and activities.
- Some teachers and some subject areas in schools and colleges have central 'homework noticeboards' where all work is posted and deadlines and expectations clearly communicated.
- 'Pop-up' messages at log-in could be used to remind learners when work is approaching.
- Some institutions set common homework patterns across all subjects so that the 'burden' of planning and doing homework is managed centrally. All too often, however, as mentioned earlier, many institutions assume that older learners do not need this. This might not be the case.

Homework tasks themselves do not necessarily have to follow a week-by-week pattern. They do, however, need to be regular. Learners need to understand and expect the pattern and homework needs to be seen to be essential and 'normal' and 'necessary'. Within this, however, it is possible to work on both *long-term* and *short-term* homework tasks and deadlines and perfectly possible, with careful set-up and clear communication, to run both long-term and short-term homework alongside each other for the same group.

Table 6.2 Short-term and long-term homework strategies

Short term	*This sort of homework is usually set week by week and is 'regular' – it is often built into starter activities in lessons.* Examples can include: • quizzes • reflective logs and learning diaries • essays • tests • worksheets
Long term	*This homework might be set fortnightly or monthly. The homework might be major investigative pieces of work. This homework needs regular monitoring but maybe not 'marking' until key dates.* Examples can include: • chapters from coursework • ongoing projects • reflective logs and learning diaries • working through textbooks and other longer sources • building elements of a play, performance or building a product

As with all homework, variety is stimulating. However, whereas variety of task is stimulating, a regular pattern and routine to allow considered time management is also essential for learners to be able to plan their time and own well-organized and meaningful homework routines.

Conclusion

In this chapter we have suggested that developing the appropriate support for homework practices through creating sustainable and scalable homework cultures is essential. We have also argued that developing these very cultures is a question of leadership and management. Senior staff need to be involved and families need to be informed and communicated with when developing new homework structures. Peer groups and older learners need to be targeted and 'recruited' to ensure that work is of a collaborative nature and that homework clubs have a 'buzz' about them. Staff need to be encouraged to set exciting and meaningful work and learners need to be stretched and challenged.

As we said at the start of this chapter, homework is a complex business. What is important is that homework support and guidance are there to underpin homework policies and structures. In this sense we can make a distinction between support and guidance. Guidance is when we lead and direct learners and might refer them on, to somewhere or someone else. Support is when we directly help learners ourselves in a more practical way. For homework to be meaningful and completed appropriately both guidance and support need to be in place.

QUESTIONS FOR PROFESSIONAL DEVELOPMENT

1. Does your institutional homework policy need review? How would you go about this? Talk to staff and managers and think carefully about the current policy you have in place. Does it still meet the needs of staff and learners?

2. What can you do to offer support for learners in their homework practices? Can you factor in lessons at the start of the year where you help support learners with developing homework habits? You should speak to older learners (once homework increases) and explore with them the circumstances under which they do their homework.

3. Have you thought about setting up peer homework networks? Encourage older learners to volunteer a lunchtime once a week to help.

4. How will you now deploy new technology to support homework and learning outside of the classroom (see Chapter 7)? Encourage older learners and peers (perhaps the more able students identified as 'gifted and talented' (see Chapter 5) to offer help, ideas, materials, etc.

5. Have you considered undertaking an action research project linked to homework? Run a project in your school and college where you develop learners' leadership skills by encouraging them to develop more informal networks of homework support. This would be a perfect action research project (see Chapter 8).

Part 2

What do you need to do?

7   300 practical strategies for learning outside of the classroom

Introduction

In Part 1 of this book we discussed how teachers are often caught between the conflicting ideas of politicians, parents and students as to what 'good' homework is. Many teachers worry about trying out new homework ideas. In part this is due to a fear that these tasks may be misunderstood, or poorly coordinated may not be carried out. Yet in part this is down to habit. None of this need worry you if right from the very first lesson you experiment with new ideas that capture and sustain the interest of learners. They will quickly associate your homework ideas with purposeful learning, fun and curiosity and will be open to all sorts of ideas rather than seeing homework as a chore, a finishing-off activity or even worse – a punishment. Stay locked in habit and your ability to excite, motivate and bring about their enhanced learning will be severely restricted.

In this, Part 2 of the book, we provide 300 ideas for you to experiment with. These ideas draw on the theories, debates, concepts and evidence based practice that we have examined in Part 1. These ideas are also based on our experience and enthusiasm as teachers and teacher educators along with the experience of those teachers we have been privileged enough to observe on our many visits to over one hundred and eighty schools and colleges in the Greater London Area. The 300 ideas that you are about to read are split into ten categories drawn from educational theories, emerging technologies and our own particular interests in education. As most of these are ideas for 'learning outside the classroom' in a more general sense, they could also be used not as *home*work as such, but for extension work, revision or private study. Equally, the majority of these strategies are ideas for homework, but some strategies take ideas for homework and then further spell out how they might be built upon in class. Also look out for the icon ⚐ when thinking about starter activities and the links between the starter and the homework. This point is elaborated further below.

Personalization and differentiation are about planning lessons and adapting teaching processes in order to meet the learning needs of all learners. Learners are different due to their education, psychology, physical characteristics, culture, gender – the list is endless. The following strategies for learning outside the classroom will automatically differentiate by task (meeting their individual needs and learning preferences by providing different audiences/activities for them to engage with) and by outcome (allowing different results and outcomes for different pupils according to activity). However we would encourage you to take on board the following golden rules when considering what homework activities you set, when and how:

- Ensure that a number of your homework strategies are ones that can be used as 'starter' activities and immediately peer assessed. The immediacy and relevance of this sort of activity will raise its profile in the minds of your learners and ease your assessment workload.
- Devise a checklist of activities you use and want to use and aim to introduce a new one every week.
- Make sure that you use a range of resources (even text books can vary enormously in the sorts of activities they offer to learners).
- When creating handouts make sure that you fully utilize your word processing abilities; borders, boxes, speech bubbles, etc. can make a huge difference to the ways in which learners respond to the homework tasks you set.
- If you are using paper and not exercise books with your learners, try, whenever possible, to use different coloured paper for handouts. You could colour code this – all the same skills or the same sub-topics could be on the same paper. Visually this can make a difference to how resources appear and can be invaluable to learners in terms of their organizational skills and when they revisit these activities for revision many months later. (Note that for some learners however, such as those with dyslexia or visual problems, certain colours of paper can create difficulties in reading the text.)
- Engage with some of the emerging technology your students almost certainly use on a daily basis.
- Finally, liaise with colleagues to ensure that you are not overloading learners with too much work at any one time (or overloading your own marking schedule).

We hope that you find the following strategies useful and we would welcome any thoughts and feedback you have on how we can improve these ideas in the future.

BEST PRACTICE – USING HOMEWORK AS A STARTER ACTIVITY

The homework ideas in this section accompanied with the icon ⓡ can be used to create starter activities for your lessons. Homework completion rates can be boosted significantly if learners see the relationship between homework and classroom tasks. The starts of lessons are ideal for this particularly if those activities involve learners working together, e.g. through the creation of quizzes, bringing in artefacts, taking pictures, etc. Assessment can be strengthened further when combined with effective questioning strategies by the teacher to ensure that tasks have been carried out successfully.

 **See it! Strategies 1–30**

Why does this matter?

To what extent does your subject rely on the ability of learners to work with visual sources (e.g. photos, statistics, diary extracts, letters, etc.)? To what extent have you asked your learners if they prefer to work with more visual learning resources? Using a variety of different resources can make subjects come alive for students, enabling their motivation in your subject. We know from educational theories that many students tend to engage and remember information better if they are working within a particular medium be that visual, audio, etc. The following strategies emphasize more visual approaches to learning while embracing a range of other learning styles. We have avoided including more obvious strategies including note taking, the setting of essays, exam questions, summaries, etc., not because we do not feel these are important but rather we assume and hope that these are incorporated into most teachers' homework repertoires.

Strategy 1 – Making a spectacle of yourself

This task works well if your subject consists of theories/approaches/different perspectives on how to analyse your topic areas. Get students to make a pair of glasses. These can be as ornate and as decorative as possible but must reflect a particular approach (e.g. Marxist glasses might have words like 'class', 'power' 'inequality', etc. and might be decorated with pictures of Engels, Lenin and so on). Get students to make these at home and bring them in. Then watch the fun as they swap their glasses in class and have to argue their topic/subject through the 'lenses' of the particular perspective.

Strategy 2 – Before and after

Give students a picture related to your own subject area (e.g. a dramatic historical scene, a photo from a newspaper, etc.). Ask them to write up what they imagined took place directly before and directly after the scene in the photograph. This activity is really effective as a way of establishing the context to the theme you are introducing to your learners.

Strategy 3 – A postcard home

Using their creative design skills get learners to create a postcard with an image or collection of images related to a place with significance to your subject area. Get them to write this postcard from the point of view of somebody visiting this particular destination.

Strategy 4 – Diamond-9

This tried and tested starter is easy to re-create as a homework activity. Using Word or Publisher, instruct learners to create nine squares that can fit together in the shape of a diamond (it is always good if they have done this activity with you in class so that they understand how the activity works). In each square they must produce a contestable statement related to their subject. Students can then bring these into the next lesson and, working in pairs or groups of three, can be asked to rank statements in a diamond shape according to if they agree/disagree with the statements generated.

Strategy 5 – Verbage

Choose a character (real or fictional) related to your subject area and ask students to create a collage of that character's face. The collage must be made up of the words associated with the character chosen. In making their collage (or 'verbage') ensure that your learners work from a variety of written sources that include broadsheet newspapers, magazines and quality internet sources.

Strategy 6 – A letter of concern

Ask your learners to write a letter to a leading professional (preferably famous) associated with your subject. In this letter they must raise their concerns/doubts/worries related to a particular development, theory or discovery within the subject. In writing the letter they must refer to a range of key concepts, approaches, evidence and people involved in the development of the topic the letter addresses.

Strategy 7 – Top twenty websites

Learners must produce their top twenty websites related to your subject area. In producing this hierarchical list they must add a short paragraph by each choice to justify why it occupies its particular ranking.

 ## Strategy 8 – Jigsaw puzzle

Give each learner instructions to make a jigsaw puzzle (simply cut up laminated images from magazines/newspapers or photocopied from your text book). Provide each student with a particular theme/concept/idea so that they can then search for a suitable image to use. You want to ensure that the completed image contains within it key concepts associated with your subject so your instructions need to be precise. This can then be brought into the next lesson and each pair/group can swap and attempt to do each other's puzzle. Learners then have to guess what the concepts are and/or what the theme of today's lesson might be.

Strategy 9 – TV reviewer

Give your learners three or four examples of television reviews for the same programme and from a variety of newspapers. Wait for a particular programme that you know will be useful to them to watch and get them to write a review of it in the style of television reviewer.

Strategy 10 – Mnemonics

Ask your learners to create a mnemonic based on concepts related to your subject. You could divide sets of concepts out to different learners so that you cover all the key terms they need to know. Their job is to create a catchy mnemonic which they can read out to the class – or even better – get the class to memorize. Put to a whole class vote, the best mnemonic wins a prize.

Strategy 11 – Speech bubbles

Each learner is given a set of images to take home and look at but with people present in each photograph. Ask them to prepare speech bubbles with appropriate quotations in the bubbles and place them on the photographs (this could be done with office sticky notes if using computers/printers at home is problematic. Each learner must bring these images to class, read out their comments to the class and justify why they have chosen those words.

Strategy 12 – Designing a booklet

Using Publisher download 10 images associated with your subject area and create a booklet allowing space for the images, blank boxes to contain copy for each image, ten caption areas, a blank 'introduction' box and a blank 'conclusion' box. Give learners the ten captions they need for these images but do not tell them which caption matches which image. After they have matched and entered the captions under the correct image, their job is to write copy for each caption along with an introduction and conclusion that explains why these images are ordered in the way they are and the relevance they have for the subject being studied.

Strategy 13 – Bring in a picture

This simple activity works well when launching a new unit/subject/module. Simply ask learners to bring in pictures on the topic of the unit about to be studied. Learners can either do this without any guidelines or pairs/groups can be asked to cover a particular theme. As a starter activity – people can be put into pairs/groups to discuss/justify why they have chosen that particular image.

Strategy 14 – In the picture

Split the class into smaller groups with at least one 'gifted and talented' member in each group. Give each member of the class a photograph instructing them that one of the characters in the photo will be 'played' by the gifted and talented learner. All members of the class will prepare questions to ask their photographed colleague based on the research they do.

Strategy 15 – Colour coding key concepts

Depending on the skills requirement of the particular subject being taught, give learners texts to read (e.g. articles, chapters, handouts) and get them to highlight key concepts, theories, names, evidence, etc. in different colours. Once they have done this ask them to provide one-sentence definitions of each word they have highlighted and attach this to the text they have read.

> **BEST PRACTICE – DON'T LEAVE IT TO THE BELL**
>
> Remember that the majority of teachers set homework in the final two to three minutes of their lesson, when most young people are keen to pack up, get out and chat to their friends. This is the worst time to set any homework tasks as instructions are often ignored or incorrectly taken down. Motivation to complete tasks will be increased if you ensure that homework is set early on in the lesson backed up by clear written and verbal instructions ensuring that the rest of the lesson acts to support the tasks you set.

Strategy 16 – Google earthopologist

This activity will foster curiosity and a sense of adventure. Give students a destination and ask them to explore this with Google Earth. Get them to take screen shots of any relevant location (e.g. they could explore the slums in Jakarta/Rio, etc. from the point of view of an anthropologist/foreign correspondent). They must make diary entries on what they see and 'experience' and then report these back to the class as they display their screen shots.

Strategy 17 – Hold the front page!

Using Publisher design a mock-up front page for a newspaper and include within it a series of photographs related to your subject but leave blank any copy that might have been inserted. Tell learners that the stories to go with the photos have been wiped from the computer by accident and that the paper cannot go to print until they write new stories to match the photos. Their task is to write the stories and bring them in to class – the resulting work can be used for an exciting wall display.

Strategy 18 – Ranking statements

This very simple and effective well-used idea is similar to the Diamond-9 strategy (see above) and is one that will create raucous discussion. Get your learners to create 10 contentious statements about your subject area. They can print these off and place in envelopes and bring these into your next lesson swapping them with a paired partner. Each pair then decides on the ranking these statements have in order of agreement/disagreement.

Strategy 19 – Design a puzzle

Tap in 'word puzzles' when next on a search engine and you will find all manner of freely downloadable easy-to-create activities including crosswords. Get students periodically to create their own crossword or alternative word game but make sure this is directly linked to the unit/module just completed. You will need to cap the activity so that it does not last longer than ten to fifteen minutes. This is a great homework task that doubles up as a really useful starter activity that can be done in pairs or groups with learners exchanging their puzzles.

Strategy 20 – Sift and sort

This commonly used teaching strategy makes a wonderful homework activity that assesses knowledge of key terms and concepts. Give students 20 key terms and ask them to word process their own associated definitions. They will then need to cut these up, separating definition from key word. These can then be brought into class and your learners can swap them, and match up on their own or in pairs. Have fun by injecting competition for the first pair that gets the correct order. It is essential that your learners have sufficient information made available to them for these definitions to be written.

Strategy 21 – Guess the clip

Using YouTube or any legal film clip reservoir, ask each learner to put together ten clips of no longer than 10 seconds. Each clip they choose has to correspond to a concept related to their subject. Taking it in turns each learner plays their clip and the class have to guess the associated concept. The learner that guesses the most concepts wins a prize. Alternatively the first person to guess the correct concept exchanges places and starts to play their selection of clips.

Strategy 22 – Concept mapping

Concept mapping/brainstorming is a strategy for organizing information, encouraging learners to integrate multiple sources of information, including visual images, emotional responses and written words. Integrating these into a symbolic system helps learners organize large quantities of information while developing a range of thinking skills associated with knowledge, understanding, interpretation, application and evaluation of the topic being investigated. Setting these diagrams as homework at the end of a particular unit/module can be a really useful way of summarizing and clarifying essential component parts of any course. These diagrams/drawings can be used to generate, visualize, structure and classify ideas, and as an aid to studying and organizing information, solving problems, making decisions and writing.

Strategy 23 – All fingers and thumbs

This activity is a variation of brainstorming and provides opportunities for you to assess to what extent learners have a grasp of the key elements that make up your topic area. It also provides an invaluable (for some) way of revising. Get learners to draw an outline of their hands onto an A3 piece of paper. Get them to identify the main building blocks of their subject and allocate them to various parts of the palms of their drawn hands. They can then use the fingers and thumbs to represent master concepts and smaller concepts, etc. We have, on more than one occasion, seen students in exams holding out their hands and remembering key concepts related to their topics.

BEST PRACTICE – HOMEWORK CHART

Create and display a brightly coloured homework chart showing the names of your students and the homework activities set for the term/year. Ensure that there is enough space on the chart to clearly indicate those that have/ have not completed homework and introduce a colour code that highlights work done to a very good or good standard. Prizes can then be introduced for those students who perform particularly well within criteria you feel appropriate.

Strategy 24 – Creating posters

Posters are a fun way of engaging learners in a particular topic but quite often they are unstructured tasks with limited learning outcomes. Ensure that your instructions work in key questions/concepts/approaches that the poster must address and offer prizes for the best poster. Remember you can design online (e.g. http://www.glogster.com) creating some spectacular effects while maintaining the learning outcomes you require.

 ## Strategy 25 – The domino effect

This is another activity that checks knowledge and understanding of key concepts. Get each learner to create a set of dominoes on paper or card (for example, half of an A4 sheet with a key word/concept and the other half with a definition). This can be done manually or you can instruct them to download software that enables this to be done quickly. This activity can be brought into the next lesson, swapped with others and used as a challenging starter activity.

Strategy 26 – Death by PowerPoint presentation

Two strategies are commonly overused by many teachers and students and often carried out badly – presentations and PowerPoint presentations. But actually both can be useful if kept short and to the point. One way of doing this is to ensure that no written words are used in any PowerPoint presentation. Instruct students to present for exactly three minutes and explain that they are not allowed to use notes. They must also be prepared to take questions from their audience. These tiny adjustments to the use of PowerPoint will transform presentations and make them a much more interactive experience for all concerned.

 ## Strategy 27 – Multiple choice

Get students to create 20 questions with 20 separate sets of answers (four answers to each question of which only one is correct). When students come into your next lesson, pair them up and get them to do each other's multiple-choice tests. This activity can be varied to include homemade crosswords; true/false quizzes; anagrams, etc.

> **BEST PRACTICE – MOVING FURNITURE FOR STARTER ACTIVITIES**
>
> When utilizing homework activities as starters to lessons do not be afraid to experiment with new seating/table arrangements. Strategy 27, for example, works brilliantly if you can set up the classroom as a 'speed dating' activity and allow students thirty seconds to grill each other furiously on the questions they have created before moving them on to the next person.

Strategy 28 – Content analysis

Give students a range of newspapers that they have to buy/read over a period of time. Ensure that the theme is worthy of photojournalistic content. Get them to measure the space occupied in the paper for certain categories of photograph (e.g. pictures of sports men and women; criminality, etc.). Get them to write up their findings discussing why they believe that less/more space is given to certain topics in the media.

Strategy 29 – Photomontage

While technology has come on in leaps and bounds in recent years remember that students often enjoy being creative with 'real' artwork as opposed to 'virtual'. Give students a particular theme related to your subject area and then instruct them to create a photomontage using images from magazines, newspapers, the internet, labels from grocery items, etc. Students need to write a short description as to what and why the images represent the concept/s.

Strategy 30 – Newspaper editor

Introduce learners to one of the many publishing packages available on their computers. Get them to design the front cover of their favourite newspaper – ideally this works best with one of the broadsheets. They must pick all the stories and pictures from other sources but must write the lead article (maximum 200 words). This can be done in pairs but works best if given as a solo activity.

 **Read it! Strategies 31–60**

Why does this matter?

With computer games, cable and satellite TV, social media sites and smart phones it can be really difficult to motivate some learners to read the sorts of texts they will require to pass their courses. With so many possibilities now for instantaneously downloading information there is also a danger that surface and skim reading skills are developed at the cost of the more critical and evaluative stances that universities and employers value. The following tasks are designed to attract learners to the sorts of reading they will be required to engage with on their courses.

Strategy 31 – Human collage

Give learners a theme to research and get them to create a collage of themselves using the texts that they have found and read related to their given theme. They must construct and display their collage of themselves on the walls of their classroom. Key words in the texts they use can be highlighted in different colours to add depth, texture and pattern.

Strategy 32 – Comic strip

This strategy works well in encouraging learners to engage more thoroughly with any text you may wish them to access. Provide learners with a particular text (e.g. poem, chapter from a book, pertinent lyrics to a song, newspaper report) and ask them to turn this into a comic strip. Provide guidelines (e.g. they must use certain concepts, key names, etc.) associated with the topic being studied and limit the strip to a maximum of twelve images.

> **BEST PRACTICE – ASK LEARNERS TO CLARIFY TASKS FOR THE WHOLE CLASS**
>
> Despite the fact that your instructions will almost certainly be clear and understandable to all – really make sure that all learners are clear about what they must do. After any instructions you issue, choose a couple of students to repeat them back to the whole class to ensure that everybody is clear about what they must do, how and when.

Strategy 33 – Red tops and broadsheets

Give learners a particular story or theme and ask them to set out how it has been covered differently depending on if it is a tabloid (red top) or broadsheet newspaper. Ask students to cut out/print off and bring into the class having highlighted key features within the text (e.g. different material; use of certain key words/adjectives, etc.). Learners can be asked to create a table detailing differences in how the story has been reported, angle taken, etc.

Strategy 34 – Alternative endings

Give learners an article/story from a newspaper/book, etc. and get them to construct an alternative ending.

Strategy 35 – Alternative beginnings

Give learners the final paragraphs of the same story from different sources (e.g. newspaper; magazine, etc.) and get them to construct their version of the complete story.

 ## Strategy 36 – From music to literature

This takes a little time to set up but it's well worth it. Identify a song that has been written about the topic you are teaching and if possible choose one that may appeal to your particular target audience. Ask your learners to use the song as the basis for researching the particular topic that the song highlights. This works well when launching a new topic and can also be used as a great starter with students presenting their findings at the beginning of the lesson.

Strategy 37 – Au contraire

Give learners a text that represents a particular view (e.g. a newspaper article written from a particular standpoint) and ask learners to re-write the text from an opposing viewpoint.

Strategy 38 – Tabloid journalist

Give learners the text that you wish them to study and get them to recreate the text in the style of one of the leading tabloid newspapers, complete with heading and pictures as you see fit.

Strategy 39 – Every picture tells a story

You will need to make sure that learners have access to technology that allows them to take photographs that can be printed and displayed. Give them the particular text you wish them to read and ask them to take pictures that capture key ideas within the text. They must then select quotations from the text and place these next to the photos they have taken. This activity can be used to create fabulous public displays of students' work.

Strategy 40 – Drama kings and queens

This activity requires a little organization but is worth all the effort. Depending on how many learners you have, choose four or five key texts that have notable characters that are related to your subject. Give each group a different text (numbers will vary depending on the nature of text and characters) asking them to identify the main characters and how their particular character might 'feel' as they are portrayed in the text they have read. Set them the task to 'play' them in short scenes in the next lesson.

> **BEST PRACTICE – INVOLVING PARENTS AND CARERS**
>
> Research consistently highlights the fact that when parents are involved in homework activities their efficacy in relation to educational achievement is significantly enhanced. Try to involve parents or carers as much as possible by sending them the school or college homework policy, requesting their signature in homework diaries and so on. Consult with them and regularly inform them if work is not submitted on time or below standard and try to find out if there are any impediments to independent learning (e.g. lack of resources, learning difficulties, etc.).

 ## Strategy 41 – Top buys

This activity is actually worth doing as you move into any revision phase for public examinations. Depending on the age of your learners get them to bring in resources (e.g. text books; revision guides, etc.) that they would recommend and get them to present their top five reasons for why people should read this text.

Strategy 42 – More than the sum

With careful briefing split your class into groups of four giving each member of the group only one quarter of the particular text you would like them to read. Their job at the start of the next lesson will be to complete a mind map of the entire text. A tiny prize for the best mind map can 'up' the level of participation nicely in this activity and help produce some superb visual resources. By giving different groups different texts the collection of mind maps can become a fabulous revision resource for future exams – particularly if they are displayed.

Strategy 43 – Essay sources

Write an essay on a particular theme but include in the margins the page numbers and the textbook references of exactly where sources have been used. Get learners to ensure that they highlight the parts of the text that relate to the page number and source in the margin.

Strategy 44 – Mark it up and summarize

Give students a set reading/article/chapter and get them to highlight key words in the chapter, etc. They must bring this in and have attached to it a 200-word summary.

Students must then verbally summarize to the class the content of the article. This works best when different articles have been assigned to different groups within your class.

Strategy 45 – Reviewer for a day

For older learners provide them with a magazine/journal article related to their subject and get them to review the articles in the style of a book review from your chosen newspaper (give them an exemplar copy of a published review). You can give them specific criteria to comment on and limit their review to 300 words.

Strategy 46 – Fragmented essay

Give learners a model answer essay from an exam question cut up into smaller sections and placed in an envelope accompanied by three or four questions. Their homework is to reconstruct the essay in the correct order and then answer the questions. Ensure that the questions are differentiated for all abilities. One of the skills emphasized here is understanding the structure of well-written essays.

Strategy 47 – Spot the error

Choose a short piece of writing (e.g. article, newspaper cutting) and recreate this with 20 errors (these could be grammatical, conceptual or both). Learners have to identify as many errors as they can and reproduce a correct version of the text.

Strategy 48 – Thesaurus 1

Many learners leave full-time education having never used a thesaurus and without realizing how useful they (particularly the free online versions) are when writing essays, poems, letters, etc. One strategy is to give learners ten key words related to their subject and ask them to come up with three alterative words for each of the ten. This can be turned into an easy starter activity by pairing up learners and asking them to guess what their original words were from one of those found in the thesaurus.

Strategy 49 – Thesaurus 2

During the course of a normal lesson ask your learners to do some free writing or write an answer to a short question. Their homework is to identify ten words in their own writing and then to substitute these words with those found using the thesaurus.

Strategy 50 – What's for breakfast?

Get your younger learners to bring in their favourite cereal packet. In class they can spend part of the lesson sticking essential key words/concepts to the outside of the packet. They can take this home, keep on their breakfast table and memorize the words for a future test.

 ## Strategy 51 – Memory mind-mapping

This activity works well as any form of revision at any time of the term/semester (for example at the end of a particular unit or series of lessons). Get your learners to use an A4 sheet of paper to diagrammatically represent the key ideas, concepts, themes, people, etc. associated with the topic just learnt. They must then bring this diagram into the next lesson and swap it with their partner. Give the whole class five minutes to memorize their partner's diagrams and then in pairs they must re-create the diagram from memory and then talk this through with their partner.

BEST PRACTICE – PEER MARKING AND A HEALTHY WORK/LIFE BALANCE

While it is extremely important that your learners have adequate advice and guidance from you it is equally important that you get the balance right in terms of your own well-being and the well-being of your learners. Learners will require written feedback from you, however it is not necessary to do this all the time. Good assessment for learning can successfully take place when learners are given sufficient guided and structured opportunities to peer-mark their work and in Chapter 5 we offer lots of advice, guidance and tips on how to get this balance right.

Strategy 52 – GoogleDocs

This activity works best with older learners approaching their final exams. Create an open document that the whole class can contribute to but ensure that you follow school/college guidelines regarding internet safety. Learners are then asked to seek out thematically relevant information (e.g. articles/evidence/big names related to their subject) and upload their top two links. Learners can also be asked to create a glossary collating all necessary terminology for their exams/coursework.

 ## Strategy 53 – Make your own cloze test

Cloze tests can be used for learners of all ages in all contexts and consists of a series of texts given to students with certain words blanked out which then need to be correctly inserted back in again by the learner. Differentiation possibilities exist, for example by including all the blanked out words at the bottom of the text so that the learner can then choose which word is replaced where. Strategy 53 requires a learner to create their own cloze test (accompanied by the correct answers) based around a particular piece of reading related to their course. Students then bring this into the next lesson and can swap this with their partners as a starter activity to the lesson.

Strategy 54 – Define the missing words

This task is identical to Strategy 53, however in this case in the starter activity of the following lesson learners will be required to define the missing words from the test. This therefore requires that in the homework activity learners will have had to ensure they provide their own correct definitions of each word they choose, in addition to providing the missing words.

Strategy 55 – Self-evaluation 1

One of the hardest skills to teach and embed into scholarly study is the skill of critical self-evaluation of written work. This is hard because it really does require the learner to stand back and re-read their own work and add those intellectual cues that signal where they are applying, interpreting and evaluating their knowledge and understanding of their field. One way to do this is to give back any written work recently completed (e.g. a class text, homework essay) and ask them, as fresh homework, to highlight the first word/s of each paragraph of their answers (and, if you really want to ram home the point, get them to identify a mid-point in each paragraph). Then get them to choose popular evaluation phrases or words to add to or substitute with the words they have highlighted (e.g. 'the relevance of this'; 'this indicates'; 'this can be applied to'; 'however'; 'further more'; 'following on from' and so on). They must then re-write their work submitting old and new versions as completed homework.

Strategy 56 – Self-evaluation 2

Similar to Strategy 55 and focusing on the ability to read and evaluate their own work, learners this time are asked to re-read work recently written (an essay, test, etc.) ensuring that their arguments are *empirically adequate* (i.e. what evidence have they given to support their particular argument/theory/principal?); *comprehensive* (i.e. can their particular argument/theory/principal be used in all cases under all conditions?); *logically coherent* (i.e. does their argument/theory/principal hold together?); *historically situated* (recognize that certain views may have changed over time in relation to the specific argument/theory/principal). For homework, learners must re-read their work and mark it (e.g. out of 20 with up to five points being awarded for each category). After marking their own work learners must come up with five targets they set themselves to improve on the next piece of written work.

Strategy 57 – Highlight

This is another task that, like strategies 56 and 57, helps learners develop their own ability to critically evaluate and reflect on their own work. It involves learners thinking about generic skills of their own subject area. Most subjects require students to have significant knowledge, understanding, interpretation, application and evaluation and to be able to demonstrate this in any writing they are required to do. When setting any written homework (e.g. an essay, report, summary) instruct learners to highlight, in different coloured ink, the word/s associated with each of these skill domains. Do this as part of the homework task itself and encourage this as a regular pattern in your homework culture.

Strategy 58 – Class scrapbook

This task can be one that is ongoing and can be reviewed on a regular monthly basis. Divide the class into groups and ensure that each group is responsible for creating their own scrapbook on a particular theme relevant to their studies. Over a longer period (e.g. a term/semester/academic year) each group must collect relevant newspaper, magazine and journal articles (including pictures and photographs) that represent the most up-to-date information available at the time. Prizes can be offered for the best scrapbook and learners can be chosen at key moments to verbally summarize their most recent findings. This work can then, if appropriate, become the focus for an exhibition for the wider school/college.

 ## Strategy 59 – Backwards Wordle

Learners are given a Wordle (see Strategy 289) created from key texts associated with the particular subject area being studied. Once given their Wordle learners are required to seek out appropriate articles/reports/stories that represent the Wordle key words highlighting within the text where the word is represented a number of times. This task can be given to the whole class or form part of a range of differentiated tasks at an individual or group level.

 ## Strategy 60 – Wordle quiz

Pair up learners instructing them to each find an article for their partner to create a Wordle from. Once created they must choose the ten most common words (excluding definite and indefinite articles) and create a mini-test on the definitions of each word which they then bring into the next lesson to use on their partner as a short starter test. Both text and

Wordle can then be given back to each partner to be used later as and when revision of the material may be required.

BEST PRACTICE – MOTIVATING WITH eLEARNING

We think teachers need to be cautious when it comes to 'truisms' about eLearning and digital literacy. On the one hand we have seen many excellent and really creative social media and online tools stimulate lessons and learning. On the other hand, we are all too conscious of the digital divide limiting access to resources for some. Equally, as with the Emperor's new clothes, new isn't always better. And yet, some eLearning tools can be massively rewarding for learners to use. Here are some tips to ensure you maximize their productiveness as much as possible.

1. Ensure you have a pedagogic purpose behind the digital tool you are using – and that you are not just using it because it is new.
2. Think about how learners will access digital content, or how they will ensure you receive it from them once done. Think about how much access they might have and if needed, discuss it with them.
3. Don't assume proficiency – ensure you go through the website/tool in class as part of the process of setting the homework – this might even apply to some 'simple' internet operations such as productively searching, etc.
4. Talk to other colleagues – try and get as many groups working online/digitally as possible so more learners can informally help and support each other.
5. Use older learners from older year groups to help support the eLearning and digital literacies of younger learners.
6. Check that digital tools do not contravene your institution's online safeguarding polices and practices.
7. Finally, think about how you will mark/assess/feedback on online and digital work – and how you will make this feedback available and accessible.

See sections E-it! and M-it! in this chapter for further eLearning and M-learning ideas and strategies.

Hear it! Strategies 61–90

Why does this matter?

Many teachers and educational theorists have noted the power of audio to facilitate and support learning. From getting learners to discuss and speak to each other to recording podcasts, the power of the spoken word – received and then reflected upon – still has a massive role to play in learning. Learning classrooms are often noisy ones, and perhaps learning homework might be noisy too? While not wishing to subscribe to often simplistic and reductionist attempts to categorize learners and learning into 'types', we can still nonetheless capture sound and the spoken word for its potential to really extend learning opportunities.

Strategy 61 – Radio presenter

Split the class into groups of three and allocate the roles of producer, journalist and 'special guest'. Using one of the many freely downloadable production applications (e.g. Audacity) produce a five-minute mini radio show on a particular theme related to your subject. This could be in the form of a current affairs chat show or could be a mini-documentary.

 ## Strategy 62 – Let there be music

Music can be a powerful incentive for many teenagers when it comes to their own subject areas. At the start of any new unit/module ask learners to create a 'top 20' list of song titles that relate to your topic area. This list can then be brought into class and used as a paired quiz where each member has to guess the name of the artist behind the title of the song.

Strategy 63 – Minor re-write

Take any piece of contemporary music that is likely to be popular with most of your learners and ask them to re-write two verses of the song including key concepts from your subject area.

Strategy 64 – Jingle jangle

If students have smart phones they can access music technology that will allow them to create musical riffs and tunes to an incredibly sophisticated level. Get students to write a jingle using key concepts from your subject and if they have access to musical technology they can sing their jingle or their composed riff.

 ## Strategy 65 – Name that tune

Ask learners to record music/song extracts that can highlight different themes but get them to edit this down to only the first five seconds of the song. This edited version can then be brought into class and used as a quiz with learners having to guess the name and/or artist behind the song. Paired up or in groups learners can then guess the particular reason why the song has been chosen, i.e. what particular themes are being dealt with and their relationship to their course.

Strategy 66 – Record an interview

Taking a historical perspective get learners to interview a parent, grandparent or neighbour on a particular theme and then play this back to the class. Ensure that interviewers are prepared to take questions from the class on the particular theme of the interview.

Strategy 67 – Speech writer

Write and record a speech made by an imaginary politician on a particular theme. Alternatively choose any current or historical character related to your subject area and ask learners to write a persuasive speech taking a particular position. This can then be played back in class with students voting on which speech is the most persuasive and why.

Strategy 68 – Speech listener

Ask learners to download and listen to particular speeches of people associated with your subject area getting them to summarize the speech with a view to explaining their summary in class.

Strategy 69 – Sucking eggs

Learners will require mobile phones or any visual recording equipment for this activity. Ask students to go home and teach their parents/carers/grandparents, etc. a key concept/theme that has been taught in class the same day. The learner must be filmed by a member of their family giving the explanation and this film brought into the next lesson. The teacher can pick at random films to be seen/shown. Alternatively the activity can be backed up with a signature from the carer/parent to show that this activity has taken place.

 ## Strategy 70 – Key word classic

This activity works well at the end of a module/unit prior to examinations and in pairs or small groups of three to four learners. Identify any members of your class that can play a musical instrument. Ask learners to write the lyrics for a song (or a verse/extract) using key words associated with your subject (lyrics can also be created to an existing song). The song can be performed with the rest of the class identifying what the key words were.

Strategy 71 – Poetry slam 1

Set up a 'poetry slam' in your class: a competition where learners go 'head to head' in preparing a spoken word poem on a chosen theme. Actual organized poetry slams have many conventions associated with them, from how and where people sit to the 'clicking fingers' of the audience instead of applause after each 'reading', some deriving from 1950s and 60s 'beat poetry'; these are widely available to research if you wish to set up the 'slam' with a more formal basis. The poems are written for homework and performed in class the next lesson.

 ## Strategy 72 – Poetry slam 2

Following on from above, the poetry slam is an excellent way to introduce a new topic. Ask learners to research in advance an issue/knowledge area and each lesson, as the starter, a different individual or group could be asked to perform, leading into the 'theme' of that particular day's lesson.

 ## Strategy 73 – News 'real'

Provide links from your VLE to newsclip footage of major world events. Try to choose some from different time periods and cultures to get a sense of the contrast in tone, language and style, etc. Once learners have listened to the newsreels, ask them to do two things:

1. Rewrite the news for the modern world, 'making it real' for today's speech and global concerns.
2. Take events from the modern world, and present them back in the tone and style of these news items from the past.

This is an excellent task to make learners aware of the 'currency' of curriculum concerns and how ideas learnt today about the world in any subject are the product of the time – and different from those in the past, even if just the relatively recent past. This would take some preparation but can be used as a revision activity at the end of the year as well as being an excellent way to set up starter activities in class once the homework is completed.

Strategy 74 – Podcasting a viva

Elsewhere, in Strategy 240 below, we suggest that learners can undertake preparation for 'vivas' – questions formally asked to them by a panel. This is both an excellent opportunity for collaborative work and also to record the practice. Ask learners in pairs to record for homework their own mini-vivas.

Strategy 75 – Record a quiz

Ask learners to record for homework definitions or explanations of key ideas from your topic area. Ask them not to name the idea or make it too obvious. Take these recordings and use them as a starter quiz for the group. Those that make the recording could get points if no one can guess the 'answer' to their explanation, assuming it was a fair description!

Strategy 76 – Name the person!

Get colleagues or other learners to help you out with this idea – enlisting the help of an older year group as part of their revision. Undertake a series of recordings of people pretending to be a famous person/key thinker from your subject area. They might have to make an impression or talk as if they were from the time period of the person/thinker in question. These can then be uploaded onto a VLE for learners to listen to as a quiz for homework. They would need to name the person/guess who it was and then perhaps write or record back something further about them.

 ### Strategy 77 – Impersonate

Ask learners to choose a character/famous person/key thinker from a hat, keeping it secret. They then need to go home and make a recording of an 'impression' of them – talking as if they were the person and saying what they think about whatever they have learnt about them. The recordings of the impressions – done for homework – can be brought into the lesson and played for the group as a quiz.

 ### Strategy 78 – Rhythm revision

Take something from your topic that needs to be simply learnt off by heart – a list of terms or the order of a process or a timeline. For homework learners should develop a memory aid using rhythm to remember the list. They are only allowed to use their hands – clapping, clicking fingers to perhaps (gently!) tapping the table. They set the list to a rhythm to help them remember and then come back and perform their own unique memory aid to the class the next lesson.

Strategy 79 – Audio corner

Ask learners to record revision summaries – bits of knowledge, summaries of key ideas, definitions of terms or explanations of content or processes. These are recorded for homework and uploaded onto the school or college VLE. A computer open on these resources is housed in the corner of the classroom with some headphones, and at key moments, when in need of help, learners can access this archive in class.

Strategy 80 – Take advantage of being stuck

As learners work in the class and become stuck or confused or simply want to know more about something, ask them to write down on a poster somewhere what they wish to know. At the end of the lesson these queries are given to the whole class to research and to make recordings of – which are then subsequently distributed through the VLE. This is an easy way to both support learners and to also add to the 'stock' of revision audios through homework needed for the Audio corner idea described in Strategy 79, above.

Strategy 81 – Buddy up

Ask older learners to run a buddy support scheme for homework and revision, with suitable safety and permissions in place. You could use free telecommunication software such as Skype or phones – giving the 'buddies' access to school or college resources for an advertised period. While working on homework or revision – maybe during the day when on study leave if older groups – they can call in and use the tele-buddy service to support them with their homework. This scheme would need to be monitored and the safety of learners and privacy of phone numbers would need to be ensured before you go ahead with the idea, but it is a very worthwhile and productive piece of collaborative and peer support for learning.

Strategy 82 – AudioBoo

This social media software (found at audioboo.fm/) allows users to record short, snappy pieces of audio for others to follow and receive. You can record at the touch of a button from a smartphone with the free AudioBoo app as long as you have set up an account (also free). You could use this to feed (on an RSS feed) into a blog or a homework page within a VLE – most VLEs have the facility for the staff who set them up and manage them to allow RSS feeds from approved pages into the environment pages. This can be a means to set homework, comment with hints and tips on homework tasks or provide clarity over instructions. See the E-it! and M-it! sections later on in this chapter for further ideas on how to incorporate audio technology into homework.

Strategy 83 – Boo-back

With appropriate permissions set up in advance and a careful eye on online safety, ask learners to set up their own AudioBoo accounts. Get these feeding into collaborative pages on your institution's VLE through an RSS feed, or your own VLE might even have a means for them to record directly into it. The benefit of AudioBoo is that it is one-click from a phone and thus has the convenience associated with mobile learning (see strategies in the M-it! section for further ideas). Once set up, this can be used for homework. Learners can be asked to record specific items and upload for everyone else to see and benefit from.

Strategy 84 – The explain game

Give learners a process which they then need to describe in real time to the rest of the class by recording an audio. This audio is made for homework. Perhaps the task will require equipment, which will need to be made available to the class the next lesson. The learner records the steps of the process and the class have to follow to make sure it is right. Depending on the task the rest of the class could even be blindfolded and asked to follow the instructions step by step. Chaos often ensues in this game, but the test of the audio is if the instructions are completely clear. This is something for learners to record for homework in real time, to be played back to the class to see if it works.

Strategy 85 – Developing listening skills

While not in anyway wishing to replace active learning with passive listening, the value of 'active listening' is still important for learners and learning. As a teacher, your job would be to support learners to try to record/note-take/brainstorm/flow diagram and see what works best for them. For homework, ask them to listen to a podcast that you have made, taking care to take notes in an active way, developing their listening skills.

Strategy 86 – Develop a story-board

This is a very specific – and often underused – means to support learners with their 'active listening'. For homework, during or after watching a video or listening to a podcast, ask learners to compose a story-board. 'Compose' seems the right word here – there is something about this act that really requires learners to engage with the parts or elements of what they are learning and to listen to and deconstruct and reconstruct this. These story-boards can then be displayed as posters in the classroom once the homework has been handed in.

Strategy 87 – Close your eyes!

This is a really simple idea and one worth exploring at times of revision and formal assessment, in conjunction with other writing-based ideas. For homework, ask learners to spend less time reading and much more time speaking out loud to themselves what they are trying to remember – but to do so with their eyes closed (30:70 ratio reading:speaking). When experimenting with this strategy, learners feel that it really helps them – over time – to focus on the knowledge in question and to be less distracted. They could demonstrate this in class in the next lesson as part of the starter – taking it in turns to close their eyes and go through what they have learnt.

Strategy 88 – Audio marking

Distribute peer work (anonymously) and ask that learners record, for homework, an audio of their marking (distributed amongst the peers after), offering advice and guidance to the other learner on how to improve. They would need to be supported in this as part of the set-up for the homework with marking schemes, examiner reports and discussions on the 'rules' of how to sensitively mark each others work and provide constructive feed*forward*.

Strategy 89 – Ad break!

Ask learners to record a one-minute advert for an idea/theory/concept as if it was to be played on the radio. This might be best done in pairs or groups. They might have to add a jingle, create a 'strap-line' or a unique selling point (USP) for the ideas in question.

Strategy 90 – Marketing competition

In groups, ask learners to make radio-style adverts that directly compete with each other. This would be a great way to develop evaluation and analytical skills. Rather than record an advert describing the unique properties of an idea/concept/view they could make a more 'aggressive' advert where they take to task a competing idea, showing how their ideas are better. Groups of competing adverts could be then subsequently played to an audience and they could vote on which was most convincing and why.

 **Move it! Strategies 91–120**

Why does this matter?

It will be many years before neuroscience provides us with a complete understanding of the reasons why learners prefer one pedagogic style above that of another. From our own experience we are constantly aware of the fact that, regardless of the age or our learners, the process of moving them during the course of a taught session energizes the learning experience. The more sensory that learning experience can become, in this case by the use of touch – the more likely you will engage all your learners. The homework activities below provide a range of tasks involving the mobility of learners and their resources, providing a rich variety of learning opportunities.

Strategy 91 – Snakes and ladders

Split the class into groups and ask each group to create their own version of snakes and ladders but using themes/concepts/key people related to your subject area. Groups then swap games and play each other's versions in class. This activity can be done with a variety of other games (e.g. Monopoly, etc.).

Strategy 92 – Create a board game

Following on from the above, ask learners in groups or pairs to design and make an unique board game – not a version of a classic game, but a totally unique game. This is very challenging – especially when it comes to designing rules and maybe question cards. Strategy 91, above, offers an easier alternative to this suggestion. These would then become something for others to play for revision and an excellent resource to keep and use another time. This would be perfect to 'draw in parents' and prospective learners at open days/ evenings, etc. and other such events.

 ## Strategy 93 – Touchy feely

Ask learners to bring in as many items/artefacts as possible that might be associated with the topic being studied. Place these items in a large giant sock (or even better ask learners to make/bring one in) and then get members of the class to guess what the item is based on the sensation of touch. Alternatively ask members to blindly feel the item and then describe what they feel to the class – with a prize going to the first person that correctly identifies the item.

> **BEST PRACTICE – CONSERVING TIME AND ENERGY**
>
> Every homework activity you set creates just that extra bit of work for you so the simpler you can make procedures for its collection the better. Many experienced colleagues stand at the door of the classroom as their learners enter or leave the room with the expectation that they will hand their homework to the teacher. This is a no-nonsense process and allows you to quickly identify any homework defaulters.

Strategy 94 – Model maker 1

Split the glass into groups and get them to make a model from everyday items at home that symbolizes a key theme/topic/event/building associated with the subject being studied. Within the model learners must try to embed/symbolize five items that are associated with the topic but demand close scrutiny for their discovery. A prize can be offered for the class member or group that correctly identify what the five items are.

Strategy 95 – Model maker 2

Following on from Strategy 94, in this homework idea you ask learners to build – out of objects they have found around (rubbish, cardboard, household items) – a model which explains an idea or how something or some *process works*. After the homework has been completed, in lesson time, learners could explain it or ask others to 'guess' what the model is and what it shows. Learners could choose what they make their model on or draw from a hat (and maybe in secret).

Strategy 96 – Treasure hunt

Split the class into small groups and get them to create clues for a treasure hunt that then needs to be completed by other group members (for example, four groups create clues for four separate treasure hunts). This works best if you, the teacher, supply the 'treasures'.

 ## Strategy 97 – Spider diagram puzzle

This activity works well at the end of a particular unit and will also double up as a useful starter activity. Get learners to devise their own spider diagram (this works best if done on computer). Instruct learners to provide two versions – one with all the labels completed (i.e. with content in the labels) and one without any content (but with the content cut out and put into envelopes). Learners must bring both versions into the next lesson and then swap their diagram with a partner. They must then attempt to match the correct label with its content and can then be 'rewarded' with the completed spider diagram.

Strategy 98 – Origami

Learners can create their own origami model ensuring that they cover each surface with useful and relevant information. Depending on the particular shape they create (e.g. a paper horse) different themes can be associated with different parts of the model (e.g. key words on the legs of the horse, key theories on the body). These can be brought into the next class and used as a vehicle for paired or group discussion and comparison.

Strategy 99 – Inserting the quotation

Carefully choose a peopled photograph that can be strongly associated with the particular subject being studied. Give your students a copy of the photograph and get them to think up and stick onto the picture suitable quotes from each of the characters in the photograph ensuring that what is said has direct relevance to the subject being studied. These can then be brought into the class and stuck around the classroom for other members to look at with perhaps a prize being awarded for the most popular picture.

Strategy 100 – Degrees of separation 1

This well-known activity is converted into a homework task involving visiting a museum, gallery or any other off-site learning area with exhibited items. Learners are asked to visit a particular venue and choose seven objects of their choice, however there must be a connection between each item by concept, theme, substance, etc. (e.g. sheep shears, wool weaving implement, clothes, burial trinkets, sheep's bones). Photos or notes can be taken and brought into the next class to be distributed as the teacher sees fit.

Strategy 101 – Degrees of separation 2

This is a slightly more challenging version of Strategy 98. This time students need to make connections between item one and item two on the basis of one similarity and one difference (e.g. item one and item two may be both knives but one might be a ceremonial knife awarded to a visiting dignitary and the second might be a Neolithic item of cutlery). If item two is made from bronze then item three might be also made from bronze – but is an item of currency from a different era. This task can consist of up to ten items and if even more challenge is to be included, item ten must link back to item one. Learners can bring proof of their visit into the next lesson and either in pairs or in whole groups feed back to each other their findings.

Strategy 102 – Antiquity apprentice

This is another popular teaching strategy adapted and designed to get young people familiar with museums and galleries. Split the class into pairs and instruct them to visit a particular museum exhibition that will be of subject interest to them. Allocate to each pair the task of selecting and taking photographs of two objects they believe they can best 'sell' to their class mates. Each pair must build up a powerful case as to why their chosen item is a 'must have' item (this works brilliantly in historical contexts where the item might be hundreds or thousands of years old). Once back in class each pair is split up into the 'salesperson' and the 'merchant'. Sales staff stay by their photograph while each 'merchant' visits the other sales staff in the classroom and must choose their best three items returning to their partner who must then decide upon the best of three.

Strategy 103 – Finger spelling

Introducing learners to any number of different finger spelling alphabets is fun, educational and can open up doors to completely new forms of communication pathways. Once you have decided on which alphabet system you wish to introduce, get learners to memorize how they spell their name for homework. In the next lesson line up the class with their eyes closed and in pairs each must guess the name of their counterpart based on their ability to finger spell.

Strategy 104 – Signing

In the same spirit as Strategy 101, learning to sign can be one of the most rewarding activities and, once learnt, very difficult to forget. Set your learners the task of learning to sign their favourite celebrity's name and at the start of the next lesson, in pairs, ask each learner to find the correct answer.

> **BEST PRACTICE – NEVER LAUNCH HOMEWORK AT THE END OF THE LESSON**
>
> Remember that research indicates that most teachers set homework within the last three to four minutes of their lessons when attention levels are low and in many cases learners are starting to pack up bags etc. making it very difficult to hear instructions, deadlines etc. Ensure that homework is set sufficiently early in the lesson and that you check that your instructions have been written down and fully understood.

Strategy 105 – Build a diorama

If we believe US television these are very popular in high schools in the States. Nonetheless, they are a good idea – if not overused. A diorama is a 3D scene. In this homework example you ask learners to build a scene that depicts something – maybe a period in history, an event, a new way of looking at the world, an idea, etc. They are usually presented as if the curtain has gone up on a play and you see 'frozen in time' a snapshot from the play. These would make excellent displays for your classroom afterwards.

Strategy 106 – Slips and things

Set a relevant question from the curriculum content that would usually require a long written answer. Provide learners with slips of paper with a deconstructed answer and ask them to work the slips back together in the 'correct order'. They stick them together and bring them into the class. A variation might be for learners to then write an introduction and a conclusion. Or, alternatively, learners could have information missing on each slip which they would then have to complete. Learners can go through their answers as part of the starter of the next lesson. This task can then lead onto essay writing or a test.

Strategy 107 – Thinking hats

Much has been written about the idea of 'thinking hats' as outlined by Edward de Bono (de Bono 2009). In this approach, the skill of 'thinking' has been subdivided into six categories – each of which asks the thinker to 'do' thinking in a very particular way. This is an excellent basis for developing evaluation and analytical skills and also a sound basis for group membership and its division. Place members of a group according to assigning each a hat as a given role, or have teams all of the same hat. It is a nice idea to actually have hats for the learners to wear when doing this sort of exercise. It makes the point and after a little bit of fun does get them to focus. (The hats could be made for homework.) As a further complication, ask them to make the hats in groups adopting an approach to the group exercise according to the characteristics of the 'hat they were making. The six hats and characteristics are, to briefly summarize:

- White hat – only dealing with the facts
- Yellow hat – being positive; being optimistic
- Black hat – spelling out the difficulties with something and being cautious
- Red hat – being emotional; using feelings in your response
- Green hat – being open to new ideas and new possibilities; being creative
- Blue hat – is the hat which monitors all the others and ensures they are following their own internal logic correctly.

Strategy 108 – Game cards

Ask learners to make Q and A quiz cards. The question could be on one side and the answer on the other or on the same side but the answer would be upside down at the bottom of the card in a much smaller font. These can then be used to play revision games in class and in moments of private study. Once made by the learners, it might be worth getting them laminated to protect them over time.

Strategy 109 – Trading cards

This idea follows the card game 'top trumps' or other, more recent sci-fi and fantasy based 'trading cards' games. Ask learners to take a topic area – one that has within it lots of competing ideas, approaches, theorists, etc. – and design a set of top trump cards. The learners would need to set the categories of the 'powers' to be competed within and the relative rankings. These card sets can then be played for some fun revision, but more importantly, the act of making them is itself an act of revision.

Strategy 110 – Multi-card choice

Learners can make sets of multiple-choice question and answer cards for others to play for revision purposes.

Strategy 111 – What was the question?

Ask learners to produce revision cards that only have an answer on them. This answer could be cryptic – an image, a phrase. The game is then for other learners to guess the question.

Strategy 112 – Thinking through the eyes of a theory

Place the names of different theoretical ideas in a hat or in envelopes and ask learners to draw them out. Then ask them to choose (again maybe at random) a newspaper article or the name of an 'issue' or exam question. The learners need to then make a speech in the style of the chosen theory or perspective, using the language and technical vocabulary associated with them. The key thing is for learners to 'see through the eyes' of the theory involved when making the speech and to try to speak convincingly and with authority. The choice of specialist language used here is often the trick to this. To reward this activity, once the speeches are completed, you can choose from each one a key quotation and turn them into a wall display.

Strategy 113 – Index cards

Distribute index cards (available from most stationers and institutional stationery catalogues). Ask learners to use these to condense notes down into a revisable format. The trick is not to copy out word for word previous notes but to try to condense them down to key words or bullet points which enable the rest of the more detailed content to then be recalled.

Strategy 114 – Handy summaries

Some teachers ask learners to *make summary cards at the start* of a module or curriculum area. This might seem counter-intuitive. Yet, what this means is that learners can use text books to look up key ideas and points or research case studies and then summarize these onto handy revision cards. These can be subsequently used in lessons and added to – thus, revision notes are being made and 'owned' all the way through the learning of the curriculum area.

 ### Strategy 115 – 10 bullets

Learners often have difficulty when dealing with large textbooks of information. For some, this is why some learners end up 'cutting and pasting' their way through homework to try to apply some order to the otherwise bewildering maze of information on offer. This 'information overload' also applies to the use of the internet. As a strategy to help with this, ask learners to make lists of ten bullet points only when using textbooks, which they then bring into class and use in a variety of ways.

 ### Strategy 116 – 10 phrases

As a follow-up homework to Strategy 115 above, learners could be asked to turn the ten bullets into a simple set of ten key words or phrases. This is important – the 'working up' or 'working on' previous notes and homework aids retention and also builds ownership and understanding.

 ### Strategy 117 – Vocab. books

Many teachers distribute a little note-book to classes at the start of the year and ask them to make, organize and keep a dictionary of key ideas and concepts and a brief definition. These can then be reviewed lesson by lesson and incorporated into starter activities as quizzes or a verbal warm-up around the class, with everyone saying something.

Strategy 118 – Surroundings

Set a long piece of work – an essay or something with a number of parts to it such as a substantial handout or research from a textbook. Ask learners to complete the tasks for homework, but to do each part in a different place moving around their surroundings – maybe even just a different room in the house or if possible a different building altogether (library, café, classroom at lunchtime, bedroom, dining room, etc.). Once each task is completed, get them to reflect on their location and surroundings – smells, sounds, etc. – and to record an observation next to each task they have completed. This is a tactic to try to get learners to better remember information by associating sensory experience with knowledge. They move around their surroundings, connecting with their environment. This can aid memory recall later. In class after this homework, test the knowledge by also asking them to recall their sensory stimulus.

Strategy 119 – Pin the idea on the body

For homework set a series of questions with answers that it might be possible to summarize with a key term or conceptual idea. Set 15 in all. These could be questions from a book or a series of revision questions about previous learning on a worksheet. Also provide learners with an outline drawing of a body and number 15 different points on the body – head, left thumb, right thumb, feet, stomach, heart, nose, elbows, etc. Once the 15 questions are completed, ask learners to 'pin an answer' onto the body diagram summarizing the answer with the relevant key word. They manipulate and move the answers around the diagram placing them where they think they will most remember them. This is a really useful way to encourage learners to recall information – by recalling in turn the part of the body they associate with the answer. As a starter in the next lesson you could get them to use sticky notes and 'pin their own body' with the answers without reading them first. Or you might do this with a giant outline of a body drawn on large paper and posted to your classroom's wall.

Strategy 120 – Timed out!

The final strategy in this section is not so much something for learners to make or produce, but rather, a nice little trick to help support learners with the 'doing' of their homework. Insert into your VLE a series of timers or links to internet stopwatches. These need to be linked precisely to tasks that you are designating a time limit for. This is great for revision – learners sit at home with the VLE open; they complete the tasks and use the timers to help them. The tasks and the time available can progress as they work through them.

Think it! Strategies 121–50

Why does this matter?

Recent research and debates, often in the UK at primary level, have concentrated upon the overwhelming importance of thinking and thinking skills. Prior to this, some in the educational system have viewed thinking as an ability – some people were seen to be born with an innate ability to think 'better' or 'higher' than others. In more recent years, we have come to recognize, importantly, that thinking is a skill – the more you do it, the more you practise it, then the better you can become. It is possible to identify that there are some thinking strategies and approaches that help develop thinking skills more than others. In these suggestions we offer ideas on how to support your learners in developing their thinking skills through homework tasks. These skills, if developed, will fundamentally affect all future learning if they can be captured and maximized.

Strategy 121 – Creating your own homework

At the start of the year ask each learner to identify what their favourite or most help-ful form of homework is and carefully make a note of this. Learners can then be asked at key moments of the course to create their own homework activity agreeing with you any parameters (e.g. word length, number of questions, etc.). Ensure that learners vary their own homework strategies but that in class they can compare the outcomes, critically engaging with each other's creative engagement with the task.

Strategy 122 – Pen pals

In class pair up students and ask them to write a letter to a famous person in the past or somebody current that is related to your subject area. For homework ask learners to swap their letters and write a letter of reply addressing the issues raised in the letter.

Strategy 123 – Doodle bug

This is a memory strategy to encourage learners to think a little harder but also have something to aid recall of information at a later date. Set any written homework task that is comprised of a number of questions, sections or parts. For each part, as they write their answer down in their books or on a worksheet or paper, get learners to make a little 'doo-dle' drawing next to it. Get them to doodle against each answer – but each doodle needs to be both relevant to the answer and distinctive from the others. Recall of the doodle in class will help many learners to recall the information too.

Strategy 124 – Agony aunt

Construct a letter that is written to an imaginary agony aunt/uncle on any theme relevant to your subject area and get your learners to write replies back to you. The best replies can be read out or displayed in class.

Strategy 125 – Being a creative

Give learners the choice of writing a poem, song, mini-scene/play/script using as many key words as possible from the subject they are studying.

Strategy 126 – A letter of concern

Get learners to write a letter to a politician about an issue of concern. This can be done in relation to a current event or to an issue in the past or one that might emerge in the future.

Strategy 127 – Diary entry

Choose a famous person related to the subject being taught and ask learners to write a week's worth of diary entries for that person.

Strategy 128 – CV time travel

Give students the opportunity to create fiction that is related to your own topic and ask them to write a CV about themselves either in the past or in the future.

Strategy 129 – Dr Who

This offers another opportunity to travel into the past. Issue learners with a map (or identify a key point on Google Maps) and if possible give them a corresponding map from a previous era. Their task is to slip back in time to the same place on the map and write up their adventure referring to key concepts/items/characters, etc. that relate to your subject area and what they imagine exists while highlighting elements that have remained the same or have changed significantly. Don't forget to ensure that you also instruct your learners to return to the present.

Strategy 130 – Alternative endings

Get learners to write alternative endings to plays, books, magazine articles, poems and news items.

 ## Strategy 131 – Five unbelievable truths

Adapted from the radio programme learners have to write two hundred words on a particular person or topic and are allowed to make up as many incorrect pieces of information as they like. However they also have to weave in five correct 'truths'. This work can then be brought in and read out with class members having to identify as many 'truths' as they can from the text being read to them.

Strategy 132 – Entrepreneurial Spirit

Get learners to imagine that they have created a particular object (e.g. the telescope, the first saucepan) or theory (Einstein's theory of relativity) and get them to prepare a three-minute 'sales' pitch to dubious peers/onlookers.

Strategy 133 – Get me out of here

Learners (this can be set as a paired homework activity) have to draw/create a virtual or paper-based maze in which an individual trapped in the centre can only escape by answering questions/riddles related to the subject. Learners must create these questions (knowing the answers of course). This can be used as a starter activity by pairing up different groups of learners who then have to 'escape' by answering each others questions.

Strategy 134 – Connecting concepts

Give learners ten to 15 key concepts associated with your subject area. Ask them to create a short story using all the key words you have given them. No more than one key word can appear in any one sentence. The best stories can be read in the next lesson.

Strategy 135 – What if...?

Get learners to consider a particular event or the discovery of a particular piece of technology related to your subject and ask them to write up an account of how society might have been altered had this particular event/item not come into existence.

Strategy 136 – Teenage identities

This works nicely when taking over a new class for the first time and allows you the opportunity to access some really useful information about your learners. Get them to write a short piece (perhaps 150 words or so) about their identity. Get them to consider their class, age, gender, religion, location, ethnicity, etc. and how all of these factors impact on how they and others see themselves.

Strategy 137 – A day in the life

Ask learners to do a short piece of writing analysing their day but in doing so they must relate concepts, themes and items that are typical of the subject they are studying.

 ## Strategy 138 – Puzzlemaker

Most people enjoy doing puzzles of some description and there are now many free downloadable programmes that make creating crosswords, true/false, anagrams, etc. extremely easy. As homework ask learners to create their own puzzles related to the subject but ensure that in doing so they produce the correct answers. These can then be brought into class and used as effective paired or group starter activities.

Strategy 139 – I'm so angry!

Get learners to write an angry (but fully supported) fictitious letter to a leading profes- sional (e.g. a psychologist, physicist, etc.) putting forward concerns regarding the most recent 'blue sky' research carried out within the particular subject being studied.

Strategy 140 – Put those hats on

You might wish to use the notion of Edward de Bono's '6 thinking hats' (2009) to support thinking skills within a group context. (See also strategy 107 for some further information on the idea of six thinking hats.) Divide homework groups into the six 'hats' with a col- lective task. All members of the group will need to work on the task outside of the lesson and each learner would need to work through the problem/challenge/task using the char- acteristics of the hat in question.

Strategy 141 – Take those hats off, and put another one on

Following on from strategies 107 and 140, set an open task – something which will take some time and can be done in lots of depth. Ask each individual for homework to approach the task six times over, each time with a 'different hat' and compare the results at the end. This is excellent for setting up project work (see Chapter 4).

Strategy 142 – Using Bloom's taxonomy

Bloom (1956) is credited with the development of what are known as 'domains of learn- ing'. In this idea educational psychologist Bloom (and later Anderson and Krathwohl 2001) divides learning into three domains or areas. For our purposes here, the first domain, the cognitive, is concerned with thinking. From low to high order thinking skills, the domain presents 'thinking' as a hierarchy:

Knowledge
Comprehension
Application
Analysis
Synthesis
Evaluation

This classification scheme is an excellent organizing principle to help divide up homework tasks. Tasks and activities could be labelled for learners as a means to help differentiate and personalize learning, targeting the skills they need to develop. It would need to be explained to learners but this in itself would help them to think about their own learning more clearly.

Strategy 143 – Colourcode

Learners could complete an essay or extended exam answer for homework. They could be asked to go back over their work before submitting it and to highlight or colour code where in their answer the different Bloom's skills are (see Strategy 142 above for an outline). This type of homework is useful to inform tutorial discussions and 1:2:1 sessions.

Strategy 144 – Peer marking

Following on from the idea above, learners could be asked to mark each other's answers for homework. They could use Bloom's categories in the cognitive domain to explore the quality of the sample answer in front of them and then set 'medal and mission' targets for each other (see Chapter 5).

Strategy 145 – Building up through the taxonomy

Similar to strategy 142 above, you could use the cognitive domain of Bloom's taxonomy to order homework tasks and questions. Start with more straightforward knowledge questions, building up through the domain to finally dealing with evaluation questions and tasks at the end. Learners could even time themselves through the tasks if that was appropriate (see Strategy 120). This could be a means to organize worksheets or other such handouts or even short-answer tests and quizzes.

Strategy 146 – Being 'synoptic'

The phrase 'synoptic' refers to the process of connecting different curriculum elements together – usually across modules or subject divisions. This is an excellent skill for learners to develop and one that really aids their revision and also higher-order thinking skills. Being able to see connections above and beyond the sometimes narrow constraints of curriculum areas and exam papers is one way for learners to develop a mastery over their subject and how they are able to manipulate it. For homework ask learners to make lists of connections between topics, ideas, modules – these can be presented as posters, flow diagrams, etc.

Strategy 147 – Study groups

Organize the learners into small groups of four or five. Set them up as 'study groups' giving them well defined roles – chair, scribe, minutes, etc. (You could divide them according to the notion of de Bono's thinking hats – see Strategy 140). They complete the given task for homework – something open ended – and meet as a group with a formal agenda and minutes to present their outcomes back to you and the rest of the group the next lesson. While not overdoing it, this strategy is better for a sustained period of time where groups can really build up the work and communication.

Strategy 148 – Meta-cognition

When we talk about meta-cognition we refer to the process of 'thinking about thinking'. This is an essential skill and one that if incorporated into regular learning experiences and opportunities delivers high order thinking. For homework, ask learners to undertake a meta-cognition task whereby they answer questions not about subject knowledge and content (which might be quite low-order on Bloom's taxonomy – see Strategy 142 for an explanation of this) but rather about how they go about the process of learning. This reflection on their own learning or thinking is very useful. Questions that encourage meta-cognition might include:

- How have you approached this task?
- Why have you undertaken the task in this way?
- What do you need to do next?
- What do you need to develop?

This sort of homework would be ideal for helping learners to engage with long-term independent projects and coursework. It would be helpful for this sort of homework to then inform tutorials or 1:2:1 meetings.

Strategy 149 – Lists away! 1

This is a very simple idea and one that really helps and develops with repetition. Ask learners to make lists! Give them a list of lists to make – and get them to write out all the elements and ideas that connect to the heading. These could be exam questions or other means to organize subject content. Think about the time of year you might wish to start this, but it is worth persevering with.

Strategy 150 – Lists away! 2

Following on from strategy 149, learners could be asked to provide titles of lists for others to make. This ensures that learners have opportunities to explore their subject matter inside and out – taking the knowledge apart and linking and using it in a variety of ways. Often this process helps with the all important skill of 'synopticity' (see Strategy 146).

Chat it! Strategies 151–80

Why does this matter?

It's one thing to study concepts, learn 'facts' and write particular arguments but it's an altogether different learning experience when we activate that knowledge by discussing, challenging and debating with our peers. It does not necessarily even matter if we get some of those points 'wrong' during those learning conversations. Far more important is the facilitation of animated discussion which embeds knowledge in such a way that we can recall, understand, interpret and apply it more readily as and when we next require it. It also offers those learners, for whom reading and writing can be initially challenging, an alternative pathway for scaffolding new forms of knowledge.

Strategy 151 – Piloting research methods

If your subject area contains a research component (but actually this works well even if no such component exists) get learners to create questionnaires/interview schedules on a particular theme related to their subject. These can then be brought into class and used to 'pilot' the format of the questions, layout, etc. on other members of the class. As an extension activity (or part of their real research) learners can then carry out this research for real (subject to ethical guidelines, etc.).

Strategy 152 – Role-plays

Role-plays are a common learning strategy and can be really useful for highlighting particular areas of concern that young people may have about the topic being studied. These need to be very carefully structured with clear parameters for each learner. They can take the form of mini-plays, scenes from a film that might be re-written, courtroom dramas, and even a talk-show format. In all cases ensure that these are written, rehearsed and timed before they are presented to other members of the class.

Strategy 153 – Teaching your parents

Get learners to explain to their parents/carers what they have learnt in the lesson and how what they have learnt relates to the aims and objectives set by the teacher. As evidence that this has been done a family member can write a note to the teacher, fill out a predesigned pro-forma, sign any homework diary with comments or even be filmed on a mobile phone, etc.

Strategy 154 – Don't mention it

Learners are required to create their own concept cards for a particular theme/unit/module with sufficient descriptive content for somebody else to be able to understand the content. In groups or pairs learners swap their cards with one person being given a concept who must then describe that concept without using the actual word itself. The first person in the group that correctly identifies the concept then takes their turn in describing the next term and so on.

 ## Strategy 155 – Newspaper review 1

Allocate each learner a particular newspaper that they must take responsibility for reading on a weekly basis. At the start of the lesson choose five students to do a weekly round-up of the news based on their particular newspaper's stand point. Once a month re-allocate newspapers to individual learners so that they develop a critical awareness of how newspapers vary.

 ## Strategy 156 – Newspaper review 2

This strategy is very similar to the one above but choose specific themes for students to seek out during the course of the week in their newspaper (e.g. teenage crime; sport; unemployment, etc.).

 ## Strategy 157 – Ten point view

Get learners to watch a relevant documentary/current affairs programme or any relevant production on television or recorded on YouTube. Ask learners to produce ten bullet points that summarize the programme and at the start of the next lesson choose a small sample of the class to read out/talk through their bullet points to the class.

 ## Strategy 158 – Hot seating

Get learners to create a list of questions (but ensure that they know the answers) that can then be used at the start of the next lesson. The 'hot seat' refers to the chair placed at the front or centre of the class on which a member of the class must answer the questions posed. These can either be their own questions that they have created, or harder still, those prepared by their class mates.

Strategy 159 – Scaffolding dialogue

This activity takes a little preparation but is worth it. Create (or get your learners to create) a themed card containing the most essential information related to that theme and, if appropriate, any associated debates. Instruct learners to take the card home and explain the contents of the card to family/carers/friends inviting those who are on the receiving end of that conversation to challenge, ask for clarification, etc. Learners will be asked to explain not just the card's content, but also the discussions/themes that emerged when explaining the card to peers/carers, etc.

Strategy 160 – Key word podcast

Choose a podcast/vodcast that has particular significance to your learners' studies (ensuring it is accessible to them). Provide a list of key words that they have to identify in the recording and get them to write down the definition and the context of the key word.

 ## Strategy 161 – Every picture tells a story

This task develops learners' evaluation skills. Set learners the task of taking five pictures on a particular theme in a museum/exhibition. They must then bring in their five pictures justifying to the class/group/partner why these five pictures were their favourite choice within the context of their particular subject.

Strategy 162 – This is your life

Learners will require the technological means to film (e.g. suitable mobile phone/camera). This task requires careful consideration of the formation of groups but is also great fun and a wonderful example of differentiation. The class will be split into groups of three with person a) taking the role of researcher; person b) taking the role of interviewer and person c) a famous or significant character within the particular subject area of the learners. Each group is to produce a short 'this is your life' biographical interview with a famous person. Once produced these can be uploaded onto the school/college intranet with a prize going to the best production.

 ## Strategy 163 – Going for a song

Learners are asked to search out and upload (e.g. onto phones/computers) the first ten seconds of any song of their choice that they can associate with the previous lesson. As a starter to the next lesson, in pairs, threes or fours, other learners have to guess the songs and the connection between the song and the previous lesson.

Strategy 164 – Keeping up to date

Get learners to seek out three research studies to update their knowledge of their own particular area of interest and then get them to discuss the answers to the following questions:

- What views do they hold about the research?
- Does it tell us anything new about the particular topic?
- Who gains from publishing the research?
- Is the research ethically sound?

Strategy 165 – A bibliography for an alien

Divide the class into smaller groups giving each group initial themes related to their potential areas of interest and/or the topics on their syllabus. Their job is to create a bibliography of sources (in print and virtual formats) for an alien (fluent in English!) that introduces them to the theme/topic in hand. These bibliographies can then be displayed in the class or uploaded onto the institution's intranet for students to draw on in the future (e.g. for exam revision and research projects).

 ## Strategy 166 – Prepare a speech

Ask learners to write a speech (with the formal conventions associated with such) on a topic relevant to the curriculum area you are studying. They could take sides in a debate or prepare something more for information/review rather than debate. Prepare them for this with showing some examples of famous speeches. They could deliver the speeches in the next lesson as a starter activity.

Strategy 167 – Double talk

Get learners to make a list of factually incorrect statements (or even a mixture of correct and incorrect statements) for homework. This is an ideal revision exercise. These statements can then be said out loud and then played as a whole class game or in pairs/groups.

Strategy 168 – Happy talk

Ask learners to make a podcast on the things they have enjoyed about the course/subject at the end of the year/term/module. Get them into the habit of reflecting and encourage them to see this as an audio-log of their reflections over time. These could be then played to new learners and classes as part of the introduction to new topics or year.

Strategy 169 – It's good to talk

Ask learners to conduct an exploration into oral history using their family or family friends. Take a topic relevant to the current curriculum area and ask them to 'interview'/ talk to an older person and make notes on what they are telling them. The trick to this task is to then encourage learners to compare 'findings' in class with each other.

Strategy 170 – Act it out

Ask learners to script (and/or prepare to act out) a play demonstrating a key point of learning from the curriculum content. These might be given directly to them in pairs or groups or learners could choose from a list. The script could be acted out/recorded next lesson or even recorded as a podcast by learners as part of the homework itself.

 ## Strategy 171 – Sing a song

As a revision aid, or for the purposes of review and consolidation, learners could make up songs to help them remember or to show their understanding of a given idea or set of related concepts.

 ## Strategy 172 – A rhyme a day

Ask learners to create their own mnemonics to help them remember core curriculum content. Get learners to make these for homework and then teach them to someone else the next lesson.

Strategy 173 – Sound bite

Rather than a speech or a play, learners can create small 'sound-bites' as used by the media and often politicians and political campaigners to demonstrate understanding of key ideas. You would have to explain what a sound-bite is, and maybe show some examples on the news or from internet sources. Learners could be given a topic and asked to develop as many as they can on one issue, or draw themes and curriculum areas out of a hat in the lesson when the homework is set.

Strategy 174 – Spoken word story-board

You prepare for this homework by giving learners images which you have arranged into a particular order presented in a linear sequence as on a story-board for a film. These images, while not being perhaps familiar to them, will represent ideas or processes they have learnt in your subject area. For homework, learners have to write a sentence explaining each picture, building up a story or narrative. These are then said out loud next lesson as the images are presented on a board to the whole class.

Strategy 175 – Pecha Kucha

Pecha Kucha is a presentation format popular in Japan. In this style of presentation, 20 images or powerpoint slides are on display to an audience for 20 seconds each, on an automatic timer. Thus, Pecha Kucha presentations last 20×20 seconds, on a really challenging time-scale. For homework, ask learners to prepare both the slides/images using Powerpoint and to set the animation time to 20 seconds per slide. Also ask them to think of the words they will say out loud for each 20 second cycle (and to make sure they practise it out loud!). The presentations can then be delivered in the next lesson – maybe as a competition akin to a poetry slam.

Strategy 176 – Advertise your learning

Ask learners to make an advert – they might script/record or even film it. The advert states 'out loud' key ideas in the subject or topic area and is an advert to persuade a notional/ fictional audience to study it.

Strategy 177 – Say it loud and proud!

Ask learners to prepare short, quick and 'snappy' verbal advertising slogans which represent key ideas or maybe definitions and explanations of ideas and concepts. These could be said to the rest of the class as a quiz next lesson with the other learners having to guess what ideas/case studies/concepts they are a slogan for.

Strategy 178 – Talk to yourself

Learners might feel a little odd with the request at the heart of this practice but it is a really good idea, and one that stimulates thinking and recall later on. You will need to explain this to learners so they can understand why you are requesting it. First, set a normal homework – something you would usually ask learners to do. But this time, ask them to talk to themselves out loud as they complete it – to say out loud what they are thinking about the work as they do it. Talking and thinking to yourself out loud is seen to help formalize thought and critical thinking and helps with focusing on the task. Also ask learners to write a reflection on this experience to see if they felt it helped and would do it again.

Strategy 179 – Write a conversation

Set a task for learners where they need to do some research and find out something new – a topic as directed by you. Their answer to what they have found is then written up as a conversation between two people. Ask learners to do this formally – will all the elements expected of a conversation – and to present the answer as a script with the dialogue. This is just a simple way to change how answers are conceived and articulated to make the homework task more memorable. As we tend to think back to ourselves as conversations it also can help some learners with subsequent recall.

Strategy 180 – Real-time chat

For homework group learners into pairs or threes and set a topic for discussion. They might also need to do some reading and research before having the discussion itself. Ask learners to use a chat room linked to your own institution's VLE or maybe an online instant messenger to have the conversation and to then save and download the text as a record of it having taken place. The group/pair hand the textual record in as proof of the homework completion.

 # Revise it! Strategies 181–210

Why does this matter?

Revision periods for public examinations can often be the most productive and enjoyable phases of the teaching year. In most cases learners have covered all the material and should have some understanding of most of it. Their motivation levels will be heightened as they draw nearer to their final assessment. What greater opportunity could you ask for to introduce a range of activities to identify and hone those examination based skills?

Strategy 181 – Make a plan!

At the start of the homework session/period ask learners to draw up a realistic plan – indicating not just topics/subjects and time and dates but also what specific revision tasks and activities they will be doing. This can then be explored in class and shared amongst peers. It is useful to launch this homework task with a conversation beforehand regarding what types of techniques exist (many of which are contained in the remaining 29 strategies in this section).

Strategy 182 – Flash cards

If your subject is one in which a public examination is part of the course get students very early on in the course to start creating their own revision/flash cards. These can be done periodically reflecting various stages of the course. It is important that they look aesthetically pleasing (special prizes can be given for the best looking cards). The cards can then be brought in and used in a variety of ways (e.g. students test each other; they can be placed on an A3 laminated pro-forma you have created with specific categories, etc.).

Strategy 183 – Flash card evaluation boards

Get learners to think carefully about the sorts of evaluation categories they might need when answering examinations and how those categories can be applied more critically to their own flash cards. Get them to design on A4 landscape (can always be blown up to A3 later) a series of blank boxes (similar to those on a game of Monopoly) where learners can place their own flash cards. Get them to think of appropriate categories for these blank boxes (e.g. concepts, theories, eras). Once your learners have created these they can be blown up to A3, laminated and used in class as a card-sort activity developing the evaluative skills of your students. The boards can be swapped and used by different groups of learners depending on the content of the lesson.

Strategy 184 – Samson and Delilah

Get learners to write down on two separate pieces of paper their strongest and weakest topic areas and concepts. As a starter activity to the next lesson match learners accordingly so that they can teach each other according to their strengths and weaknesses.

Strategy 185 – Organizing student folders

Part of the learning environment you create will be comprised of the work that students bring to your classrooms when they carry out work at home. Many learners do not necessarily come 'armed' with the sorts of organizational skills required to study as they get older. Folder checks can be an invaluable way of modelling this and we strongly advise regular structured checks of their folders, portfolios, etc. as part of your homework repertoire. Ideally keep a past folder available so that students can see how best this is done (e.g. plastic wallets that are labelled, dividers, colour codes, etc.). All your learners should feel that this is an essential part of their learning experience with you. Do this activity three or four times a year. Instruct learners that for homework they are to prepare their folders to look immaculate, for example, labelled dividers, maximum of two handouts in each clear plastic wallet and so on. It is essential that this is rigorously done and taken seriously by learners. Follow up any learner that has not done this and offer prizes for the best looking folder.

Strategy 186 – Model answer

You will need four model answers for this particular revision task. Set four essay titles for homework (ensuring that you have model answers for each). Each learner must produce a plan for each essay. Students then come into your class knowing that they will write under timed conditions one of the essays but they will not know which one until you set it. Give students ten minutes in groups of four to discuss each of their plans and then choose one essay title for them to write up under timed conditions. After they have completed this 'reward' them with the four model answers and give them the opportunity (with an examiner's mark scheme) to peer mark their work.

Strategy 187 – Fool the examiner

After any timed writing that learners do for you, make sure they read through their own answers. Instruct them to highlight key words, names, evidence and so on. Make sure they also highlight the first three words of any new paragraph and their conclusions. Provide for them a list of key evaluative phrases (e.g. 'in contrast'; 'following on from this'; 'returning to the question'). For their homework they must identify which phrases they could have used in their answer. Ask them to rewrite their timed answer and to submit to you both versions – along with the list of key words/phrases they have identified from your list as appropriate.

Strategy 188 – Marking their own work

As learners move ever closer to public examinations give them the opportunity to mark their own work at home using the examiners' mark schemes. Their efforts at using the schemes will help them fully understand the examiners' expectations and they can then compare their attempt at this with others in the next lesson by swapping and marking each other's work. They should try to get as close to agreement on final marks as possible. Any disagreements can be used as a source of in-class discussion.

Strategy 189 – Make a model answer jigsaw

Prepare a model answer to an extended question and ask learners to organize the answer (presented as a series of strips) into a sensible order to make the complete response. Ask them to write a brief justification of why they have ordered it how they have.

Strategy 190 – Clozed model answer

Provide learners with a model answer presented as a cut up series of strips (see Strategy 189) but ensure that it is not a full answer. Learners have to put the model answer into the correct order and then supply the missing parts – whole paragraphs, sentences, evaluation points – to fully complete the response.

Strategy 191 – Prepare for a viva 1

A viva voca is a type of examination where learners are asked to formally meet with a panel to be quizzed verbally on their knowledge of a specialist area. Use this technique coming up to exam time. Give learners a topic, schedule a meeting time for the viva with a panel of teachers and ask questions.

Strategy 192 – Prepare for a viva 2

In a variation of the strategy above, learners themselves could also sit on viva panels, asking questions of each other. They would need to prepare these questions in advance – both the question and their own answer to it.

Strategy 193 – Cover it up!

For homework you ask learners to take some text, notes and/or previous revision materials and to read and then cover them up so they cannot see them. They need to time themselves and write out what they can remember before doing it again. They repeat this over and over and hand in each attempt to show their working out at the end of the process. This type of task might be best not 'marked' as such, but rather assessed by a 5-minute conversation for each learner ascertaining how far they got and how confident in the material they feel. This could be the practice for then moving onto being questioned about the material in a viva.

Strategy 194 – Summary summary

Ask learners to go through their notes from class and make summaries. First, they could write two or three long paragraphs, then short bullet points and on the third and last attempt just a few key words. They then repeat the process. Like Strategy 193, they could show their workings out and various attempts and have a conversation about their progress rather than the individual attempts being 'marked' as such.

Strategy 195 – Make acronyms

Rather than make a mnemonic, learners can make acronyms for homework instead. Some might favour these over mnemonics and vice-versa so when it comes to revision maybe you can allow some choice to your learners?

BEST PRACTICE – VARIETY IS THE KEY

When it comes to revision and revision homework, variety is the key. Encourage learners to try different approaches. The key to this is to structure revision homework so they encourage writing, speaking and reading, but each time with the emphasis upon learners being active. Get them to make choices over favoured methods, but to nonetheless try different methods.

Strategy 196 – Podcast revision summaries

Elsewhere we have noted the usefulness of podcasts and audio as homework tools and methods. Ask learners to record their own audio summaries and to then use these to revise from when they subsequently go over timed examination questions in class. They could post and share these within your VLE.

Strategy 197 – Voicethread

Using this online application will lead to deeper and more evaluative and reflective responses. Use the voicethread website (voicethread.com) to encourage a whole class 'conversation' about a revision topic. These could then be displayed back to the learners in class or links posted on your VLE for future use.

 ## Strategy 198 – Use your own words

This idea is so simple – but lies at the heart of all learning and also all good revision. For homework, students take ideas, topics and knowledge and simply write it up again in their own words. They make a series of lists – limit what they write to four sentences per 'idea' – and hand these lists in. By forcing learners to manipulate their own language, you (and they) can easily see what they have truly understood. They can test each other on what they have come up with at the start of the next lesson.

Strategy 199 – Chunking

A great deal of psychology research into memory advocates the use of 'chunking' (which we deploy in Strategy 200 below). Chunking refers to the practice of grouping and breaking down information from a longer block or series into smaller groups – groups of four or five usually work best. So, learners do not learn 15 things to know about X, but instead learn the first three, then the next three, then the next three and so on, 'chunking' down the information to make it more easy to handle cognitively. Ask learners to go through their notes and even their shortened revision notes (see Strategy 194 for example) and divide the information into reorganized chunks. Groups of four or five 'bits' of information work best here. Get them to write them down or to record their own audio summaries of these chunks. This will aid memory of them.

Strategy 200 – Hooks

As well as the process of 'chunking' (see Strategy 199 above), creating 'hooks' is another well-recognized means to aid memory and recall of information. A hook is a word or phrase which you can then 'hook' onto further chunks of information. It is something – a handy aide memoire – that can then represent longer ideas and words. After making chunks of information (putting revision materials into clusters) for homework ask learners to give a name or 'hook' to each chunk or cluster to make them easier to recall.

Strategy 201 – Bag it

In language teaching (and in some other subject areas) use is sometimes made of 'language bags' – words which learners draw out of a hat and then do something with – define, explain, provide alternatives, give opposites for, and if modern foreign language teaching or ESOL work, maybe translate, etc. But there is nothing to say other subjects can't have their own language bags. You can make them and loan them to learners to revise with, or you could ask learners to make them themselves. Fill them with key ideas, technical words, concepts and common words used in examination answers.

Strategy 202 – Be selective!

This is a very simple idea and can easily be combined with other strategies in this book, maybe as a warm-up or a precursor. Provide text to learners (that they can write on) and ask them for homework and revision to select and highlight key bits. You could provide further 'rules' here to refine the idea – the ten most important facts, or only the points of comparison with X, or only evaluations of Y. This is a very quick and easy way to get learners to start to make choices and be selective over content.

Strategy 203 – Make quiz cards

Ask learners to make quiz cards on a given topic. They would have both a question and an answer – one on one side and one on the other. For revision family members and also other peers can test learners using the cards.

Strategy 204 – Wallwisher

This Web2.0 online tool can be found at wallwisher.com. It is an online noticeboard where others can also post ideas and suggestions. Set up wallwisher noticeboards by revision topic and for homework ask learners to contribute as much as they can to each. You could structure this to take place throughout the year or divide the topics amongst the class. If you are going to use free online tools such as this, ensure you check with your institution that they are accessible on-site and do not break online safe-guarding protocols in your organization.

Strategy 205 – Sticky notes

Ask learners to write a plan for a longer-mark examination style answer, but to put the points on sticky notes. They could write both a key word for each point and also indicate the content of the point. Get them to number the points/sticky notes in the order they would write them and finally ask them to write a very brief justification of why they have ordered the answer in this way. As they are on reusable sticky notes, they can be brought into class, and with the aid of peers, moved around in different ways and in new combinations once peers show their answers to each other and work collaboratively.

Strategy 206 – Only if . . .

This takes some explaining to learners and some setting up/preparation in class but the rewards are often very rich, developing some useful application and evaluation skills. Provide a worksheet to learners for revision with scenarios on. Things that might happen or outcomes of research/events/case studies they have already learnt and should be familiar with. Each of the scenarios should only be able to exist if underpinned by a further, earlier series of conditions or prior events. Thus, the learners need to identify what these conditions are – only if X or Y would occur first.

Here is a simple example:

A kettle boils
Only if . . .

The answer(s) might be –

It is plugged in
It has water
It was switched on
There is electricity available
The element is working

You would need examples from within your curriculum area. This is a very simple tool once you get the hang of it and can explain it to your learners. It very quickly encourages learners to think about connections and conditions.

Strategy 207 – Revision comics

This particular activity might be best earlier on in the year, and not left until the 'revision period' as such. There are many 'comic making' applications and websites currently available. An internet search will show you which ones are free and which you might need to purchase institutional subscriptions to (if resources allow). The homework would be for students to make their own revision comic - images and text summarizing ideas, case studies, essay debates and even whole topics.

Strategy 208 – Word mats

Word mats are not a new idea and a quick internet search should provide you with examples, maybe even from your own subject specialism. Sometimes teachers make these for learners, but it is better for learners to make them themselves. Put simply, a word mat is a single sheet summary of all key words and concepts for a particular curriculum area/topic/model listed and categorized or grouped in particular ways. Once made it thus provides a single quick-look summary of all the associated technical words. This is not to be confused with a mind map although the process of creating them and the benefits for the learner might be similar. But once created, they are perhaps more useful than mind maps when revisited.

Strategy 209 – Commanding attention

Command or trigger words (compare, outline, define, evaluate, to what extent, etc.) are part and parcel of the very fabric of examinations and exam questions. Yet many learners do not understand what these command words mean and what implications they might have for the response required in the answer. For homework provide learners with a list of as many different commands/triggers as you can and ask them to define and explain them. You could provide this as a worksheet.

Strategy 210 – Play an online game

The BBC schools website (www.bbc.co.uk/schools/games) has a large resource of online revision games to play. These are organized according to subject and are suitable for a wide range of learners and age ranges. Investigate the site yourself, setting the games you think are appropriate for your learners.

Research it! Strategies 211–40

Why does this matter?

Being a researcher provides an invaluable opportunity to gain deeper understanding of the subject and develop the sorts of skills that employers and universities cry out for in young people after they leave school or college. There's nothing quite like going out into the 'field' to develop deep knowledge and understanding of any discipline. For many, the coursework, project, piece of fieldwork or mini-thesis will be the catalyst for later research at university. The following strategies are designed to generate interest in becoming a researcher and some of the generic skills that this activity requires.

Strategy 211 – Cost benefit analysis

Write one or two paragraphs (more depending on the age cohort of learners) on the costs and benefits to society on a given piece of research related to their subject area.

Strategy 212 – Starting that research diary

Get learners to create their own research diary to log or record problems and issues with their research right from the very beginning of their research project. This can be used to jot down any initial brainstorming of ideas about what they might wish to research, any problems they encounter, and any useful information sources (e.g. YouTube clips, websites, magazine or newspaper articles, books, etc.). Get learners into the habit of updating this on a weekly basis. They can start by answering the following sorts of questions:

- What topics really interest me and why?
- What sorts of research methods might I really enjoy using?
- What issues have arisen in the news that interest me enough to want to research a related theme?
- Is there anything in my own biography that makes me curious enough to see if others share similar experiences?

Strategy 213 – Scrapbook

Whether or not this scrap is real or 'virtual', starting a scrapbook at the beginning of the year can be a fantastic scaffolding activity for research later on. Regardless of what subject area you teach identify a particular theme or themes and allocate these to individual learners or groups of learners. Their job throughout the year is to collect photos, stories and articles on their particular theme. Ensure that they include items from broadsheet as well as tabloid newspapers so that they develop their critical thinking. Out of this scrapbook can emerge a series of themes/research questions, etc. that can be developed into research projects at a later stage. The best of these can be exhibited in the library for future reference by other learners.

Strategy 214 – Methods vocabulary dominoes

Because this homework activity takes time it works best when your class is split into groups of three but you can decide depending on the size of the class and the amount of terminology you want to introduce. Give your learners a list of all the methods they need to know about before choosing and embarking on their research. Ensuring you provide them with an example, instruct each group to create a set of card/paper dominoes made up of the names and definitions of different research methods. In the next lesson get the groups to swap their dominoes and play the game as a starter to the lesson.

Strategy 215 – Sampling vocabulary dominoes

This is similar to Strategy 214, but this time the dominoes are made up of the various sampling strategies, and the definitions that your learners will need to be familiar with.

Strategy 216 – A methodological treasure hunt

The feasibility of this task will largely depend on what sort of institution you are working in and where it is located but this is great fun and a lovely way to generate enthusiasm, knowledge and understanding for some rather dry methodological terms. As homework split the class into groups getting each member to revise their knowledge and understanding of the key terms in preparation for a treasure hunt. Carefully choosing the most appropriate key methodological concepts create a treasure hunt with clues that draw on key studies, methods and sampling strategies ensuring that there is some suitable 'treasure' at the end of the hunt.

Strategy 217 – Methodological true/false

Get learners to create a true/false quiz based on methodological terms they require when carrying out research. Ensuring that they also supply the answers they can bring these into the next lesson. Set the class up with two rows of chairs facing each other and give each pair 45 seconds to fire the questions they have prepared at their opposite number, who then does the same. After 90 seconds move one row down one person and then start the quiz again for a frantic but fun starter that builds on homework and the terminology required for research skills.

Strategy 218 – Building on existing research skills

Using their research diaries get learners to write a short piece on the existing research skills they already unknowingly possess. Get them to think of any everyday activity they might have been involved in, for example, buying a new mobile phone, helping to organize a party or trip and so on. They must list exactly what they had to do and what skills they deployed (e.g. time management, use of the internet, etc.) and then identify in what ways this might be similar to researching their own topic area.

Strategy 219 – Comparing research methods

Pair up learners and get them to decide on a particular common theme of interest. They must jointly produce a short questionnaire and a short interview schedule on the same theme (after seeking appropriate institutional approval) and decide which member will use which method. The pairs then go out and deploy their questionnaire/interview schedule on three people before coming back together again to compare findings and the advantages and disadvantages of the two research methods. This activity can be adapted for different methods and different group numbers.

Strategy 220 – Replicating other studies

Set learners the task of finding one key study related to their own subject area that is of particular interest to them. It does not matter how large scale the study is but the task is to reproduce a plan for their own much smaller study based on the original famous study. The study must be 'doable' – and can, for example, play around with different variables (e.g. gender, class, location, ethnicity, age, etc.).

Strategy 221 – Research proposal

Get learners to write a short (between 100 and 300 words in length depending on age range) proposal for a piece of research they might carry out in your subject area. Ensure that this has structure to it and get them to think about the practical, ethical and perhaps theoretical issues they might need to consider when carrying out such research.

Strategy 222 – The Today programme test

Students in pairs must present a two-minute role-play imagining that they are successful university professors being invited onto the BBC to explain the findings of their research to a radio journalist. Two minutes is all they have as that is the time slot allocated to them on the programme. They must take it in turns to interview each other role-playing the researcher and academic and answering the following questions:

- What is the research about?
- How was it carried out?
- What difficulties were encountered during the project?
- In what ways have we gained by having this particular research carried out?

Strategy 223 – The ethics committee

Write a letter of complaint to an imaginary ethics committee about a piece of research carried out in your subject area. Consider the ethical issues really carefully and structure the letter around each of these issues (e.g. harm to others, consent, relationship between the researcher and the researched, etc.).

Strategy 224 – Spot-the-ethical-error

While this activity will take a little while to prepare you can use this again and again so it is worth the effort. Write up a fictitious summary of a piece of research but build into it a number of ethical errors (e.g. including the real names of the respondents). Give this summary to your learners and get them to identify all the mistakes and how they could have been avoided.

Strategy 225 – Cloze values activity

Create a short cloze activity that focuses on the role that values play in research design and implementation. This text can be differentiated, for example, by including all of the missing words at the bottom of the text.

Strategy 226 – Research diary and methodology

Once the learner is slightly clearer about the research methods and/or their research methodology get them to write a short piece in their diaries briefly answering some or all of the following questions:

- Why is their choice of method/s the most appropriate for their study?
- How will they carry it out?
- What potential problems can they predict (e.g. practical, ethical, theoretical, etc.)?
- How might they solve these problems?
- How will they gain access to their sample?
- Why did they reject other methods?

BEST PRACTICE – CREATE A HOMEWORK BOX

Try creating a designated homework box where learners must place their completed homework activities. Ensure that you remove the box at a pre-agreed time with the outcome being that any 'late' arrivals will have their work marked 'late'.

 ## Strategy 227 – Spot the mistake

Get each member of your class to design a 20-part questionnaire related to their research interest but ensuring that they make 20 mistakes specific to poor questionnaire design (e.g. one error might be to omit a box where the respondent can place their tick, etc.). This can be then brought into the class to be 'piloted' with a partner as a starter activity ensuring that the mistakes are then clarified.

Strategy 228 – Quantitative and qualitative approaches to research

Put together a list of ten titles of research projects (you could make these up or draw on existing research within the topic area being studied). For homework, learners need to decide and justify on which approach – qualitative or quantitative – best suits the title of the research project justifying all their choices.

Strategy 229 – Hypotheses and research questions

Give learners a list of five exemplar hypotheses and get them to turn each one into three different research questions.

Strategy 230 – Hypotheses, aims and objectives

Give learners a list of three hypotheses and three aims (all unrelated) ensuring that these are jumbled up. Instruct your learners to identify which are hypotheses and which are aims. Then ask them to choose any two suggesting a working title for the project accompanied by two objectives.

Strategy 231 – Carrying out an observation 1

Carrying out a method of research for the very first time is very different from just reading about it and is a rich learning experience for those about to embark on the ins and outs of research methods. Ensuring that your learners have been fully briefed on the various types of observation, the methods for recording what they see and ethical considerations, set them the task of carrying out an observation for only five minutes. Choose the location carefully by ensuring that there is a wealth of data available to them to record their observations (e.g. in a busy shopping mall; at the entrance to a busy station).

Strategy 232 – Carrying out an observation 2

For a slightly more ethnographic observational experience, pair up learners and get them to visit each other's houses when both families are engaged in a particular activity, e.g. a Sunday meal, shopping trip, etc. In both cases meticulous observational notes need to be recorded (either in quantitative or qualitative formats) the results of which can be compared by the pair and fed back in either written form or as part of a classroom discussion.

Strategy 233 – The importance of key words

One of the most useful skills any budding researcher can master is understanding the importance of key words when searching online. Give your learners an exemplar topic in which you have given them related key words allowing them in class to carry out that search to see what they come up with. In pairs or threes get them to work on their own topic areas identifying their top five key words. Their homework is to assess which of their five key words generates the most effective and useful sources for their research.

Strategy 234 – Qualitative interviewing

Some learners find it really difficult to understand the justification for small-scale, qualitative approaches to research such interviews. Choose a particular topic in which statistics are used within the media to create a particular narrative, for example the unemployed, immigrant workers and so on. Set your learners the task of carrying out a single interview with somebody that they may know that fits within one of these categories with a view to exploring how interviews can offer valid, authentic and in-depth understandings of particular social phenomena.

BEST PRACTICE – OFFERING LEARNERS A CHOICE

Offering learners a choice in activities is a powerful way to communicate your openness to their learning preferences which in turn can feed into rising levels of motivation. While we do not suggest you do this every time you set work, carefully chosen activities where choice is available will endear you to your students and influence their overall perception of the value of the work you set them.

Strategy 235 – Designing a quota

Understanding the complexities and justifications for different sorts of sampling strategies can be really challenging for young learners new to research. In this activity get your learners in pairs to design a quota for a sample of 50 students aged 16 or over in your school or college. The selection must take into account the requirement for a cross-section of students for a piece of research exploring their attitudes to homework.

Strategy 236 – Four methodological golden concepts

As concepts, reliability, representativeness, generalizability and validity are often a source of confusion for those new to research. Carefully choose three exciting pieces of research related to your learners' disciplines and get them to identify which of the three studies reflects these characteristics and why there is variation between the three.

Strategy 237 – Coding qualitative data

It can be really hard for those new to research to understand what is meant by analysing data. Get learners in pairs to find and agree on a published interview with one of their favourite celebrities. Make sure that the interview they seek is of a suitable word length (i.e. over 250 words long). Get them to 'code' this by a line-by-line reading where they jot down initial words in the margin that summarize their thoughts sentence by sentence. Make sure that each pair does this individually at home and then brings this into your next lesson so that they compare their initial 'readings' of the data.

Strategy 238 – Photographic content analysis

Ask learners to choose a particular theme of interest to them within the media (e.g. gun crime, celebrity culture). Their chosen theme needs to be one that is currently available to them and represented through photographic journalism. Get learners to survey different newspapers (e.g. two red tops and two broadsheets) cutting out and measuring the photographic space taken up in the newspaper on a particular theme (e.g. gender representations of athletes). Get them to bring their chosen photographs in to examine why this might be a useful form of data collection.

Strategy 239 – Alternative interview stimuli

Researchers use all sorts of methods to engage people in conversation. This activity gets learners to think about the best ways to engage in qualitative conversation. Split your class into fours and ask each pair to experiment with two different methods on a particular theme, for example, the characteristics of a successful athlete. The first pair must create ten images representing different traits (e.g. muscular, tall, etc.). The second pair must create ten cards with single words on (e.g. 'female', 'powerful', etc.). Then ask each group to approach individuals getting them to rank both sources in the order they prioritize. In class each group can feed back on the sorts of conversations these research stimuli generated and their advantages and disadvantages as a research tool.

Strategy 240 – Preparing for a mini-viva

Shortly before completing their final project ensure that your learners are aware that they will have to prepare and carry out a five-minute presentation on their research project. This presentation should be a relatively formal affair in which they present to one or more teachers (alternatively the 'panel' could be made up of older, more experienced students). The 'viva' should allow the opportunity for the learner to present the aims, methodology, findings and conclusions but also provide an opportunity for the panel to pose formative questions. The aim of the viva is to formatively fine-tune any remaining issues that the student can solve prior to handing their work in.

 ## E-it! Strategies 241–70

Why does this matter?

As we have said elsewhere in this book, we feel that teachers need to be cautious of reliance upon eLearning tools and approaches without appropriate support, access and pedagogy behind them. And yet, when used well – and for the right educational reasons – eLearning and digital content can provide a rich source of very motivational homework opportunities. Most schools and colleges have networked learning infrastructures – VLEs. These offer rich possibilities due to the increasingly sophisticated and interactive tools and plug-ins they have.

Strategy 241 – Online chat

Ask learners to participate in an online synchronous (in real time or 'live') webchat. Sometimes these are called not seminars but 'webinars'. Many VLEs offer these tools as part of their basic infrastructure although you might need to group the learners or even give them permission or 'add them' to user groups. Set up a topic for debate, ask learners to think about it and do some research, and then 'meet' online at an appointed time to discuss what they have found out. You will need to monitor and measure interaction and participation and often these tools provide this analysis by user for you. This could be a great way to set up a revision or homework club throughout the year.

Strategy 242 – Post it

While working asynchronously (not in 'real time') learners can contribute posts to forums or discussion topics within most VLEs run by schools and colleges. You will need to be clear about the rules here – number of contributions, length of contribution, etc. Embed these practices as part of your regular homework cultures then perhaps you do not need the rules and can allow and support participation and interaction in a more ground-up organic fashion, being directed by the learners themselves. Set the topic for discussion and paste and archive the best contributions to turn into revision notes for groups later on.

 ## Strategy 243 – Ask, ask ask

Most VLEs have the ability for learners to pose questions. You will need to be creative regarding where these are posted and what the questions might be called – it might be in a dedicated FAQ section, or perhaps as regular threads in a forum post. Encourage homework learners to ask questions about things they do not understand or are stuck on. These can then be addressed in the next lesson either by yourself or thrown open to the whole group – an ideal starter activity.

Strategy 244 – Pin with interest

Pininterest is a social media platform (see pininterest.com) that allows 'blog-like' posts to be shared to the community on online 'pinboards'. Many teachers have found that the simplicity and rich visuals of this online pinboard can really help learners to see information quickly and clearly. Think about using one for homework – an archive of ideas, questions to work through – or even ask learners to make their own in place of perhaps more traditional written responses to homework tasks and questions.

Strategy 245 – Infographics

A quick internet search of this term – 'infographic' – will expose to you a rich array of dazzling online posters which take information and data (including numbers and statistics) and allow the user to create stylist posters and graphics to illustrate a complex idea but in an easy to understand and engaging way. Another quick internet search of infographics for teachers will provide you with many examples of how teachers are using these in their teaching – and asking learners to create their own. This would be a very engaging homework task, with appropriate support in place and some considerable set-up in the class beforehand.

Strategy 246 – Text2mind

This is a very simple and useful web tool (text2mind.com) that allows users to create mind maps in a very easy to use way. The online tool gives the user considerable and highly intuitive control over the ordering and 'indenting' of points which then control the spread of the mind map and help with which points 'grow' out of which others. You can also draw the finished mind map around the screen until it all fits and has a suitable and pleasing shape. This is an ideal tool for learners to use, and an ideal homework task. As with using other online tools such as Wordle have a think about how you will ask learners to save their finished creations and get them to you for you to assess.

BEST PRACTICE – THE FLIPPED CLASSROOM

We use the term 'flipped classroom' to denote how use of the internet and online, digital tools and social media can 'flip' or reverse the centrality of the teacher in the classroom, placing emphasis upon the learner and their interaction with others and their learning. Thus in flipped classrooms learners use online tools for homework and come into the classroom fully informed. They can use online tools inside the classroom if they are stuck, need extension or need to understand something while the teacher is busy helping someone else. The internet is seen, in this philosophy, as a major contributor to, and enabler of, learners' independent learning. Using VLEs, social media and digital tools for homework is one step in the direction of this flipped classroom if used well and productively.

Strategy 247 – Ning communities

If you do not have access to a VLE but wish to engage with learners in an online community as part of homework practices then you might wish to explore Ning. Many teachers have used Ning communities to great effect. Ning provides some simple levels of interaction that some VLEs might not, so there might be an argument to be made to use both. Homework tasks can be set, done and assessed all within the online community itself (although this is true of any online forum, discussion board, etc.). Homework tasks can be shared and discussed even if the homework itself is something more traditional.

Strategy 248 – Post post post

For homework ask learners to make posts and comments to blog posts that you have set up. Provide links to videos, audio and newsfeeds and then learners might need to go online and respond to them accordingly. This is very useful if your subject requires a sense of current affairs/news. Undertake this either within a managed VLE or an external blog.

Strategy 249 – Search light

For homework you ask learners to make a list of search terms they have found on the internet that have led to useful information on a given subject. They also need to write a justification of the sources they have used and explain how they know/think they are trustworthy and credible.

Strategy 250 – Cut and paste

Many teachers would recoil in horror at asking learners to cut and paste from the internet – and quite understandably and rightly so. But with the accompanying caveat, cutting and pasting from the internet can be used as a genuine learning opportunity. For homework ask learners to use the internet to research a given topic. Ask them to cut and paste their findings into a word document but to indicate where they got their information from. This might also be combined with the 'search light' strategy above. Then – and this is the vital point – get them to start to 'chunk' the information down into their own words. Ask them to first highlight the key points, then to write it out in their own words and then to identify key words. By the end of these three easy steps you and they can judge if they have understood it – and not just uncritically cut and paste it.

Strategy 251 – Pop quiz

Many VLEs have the functionality for quick short-answer quizzes – sometimes multiple-choice – which can then be 'marked' for the learner as they go along. Set up some of these and ask learners to complete them for homework. Remember to differentiate the difficulty of the quizzes or ask some leaners to do more of them than others.

Strategy 252 – Mark online

Using school and college VLEs to share documents between learners is an easy and paper-less way to get learners to support each other – and to formally set this up for homework purposes. Ask learners to complete an exam answer and to upload to a central place. A peer can then mark and both peers can compare their answers together. Following this, ask learners to make five suggestions for how the other can improve.

> **BEST PRACTICE – LITERACY, NUMERACY AND NETRACY**
>
> Most teachers recognize and understand the need to embed numeracy and literacy in their teaching. But how about 'netracy' or what is called 'digital literacy'? Think about how you will prepare learners for using the internet to do their homework – even for basic searching. Do not take for granted supposed 'digital nativeness' of learners and do not think that immersion and familiarity with social media and online worlds means that learners can use these critically and efficiently. Provide them with examples, walk-throughs and screen shots and show them how to use online tools and the internet in general.

Strategy 253 – Picture picture

There are many social media sites where you can find free-to-use pictures. Make sure you direct learners to sites which advertise that they are copyright free. Learners can use these pictures as part of their homework to make collages and story-boards to explain an idea or a process.

Strategy 254 – Go and animate

The website goanimate.com provides a free service to allow users to make their own animated videos. This would require careful set-up and also a clear remit – the need for information to be presented as an animated video and not in a more traditional format would need to be thought through, but the website is very easy to use with some practice. This would be an excellent approach to take if learners needed to make stories, narratives or descriptions of events and case studies for homework.

Strategy 255 – Reflect

In visiting schools and colleges as part of our teacher education role we are becoming increasingly aware of teachers and trainee teachers taking advantages of blogs, wikis and forums within VLEs to ask learners to keep homework reflective logs or diaries after each and every lesson where they document what they have learnt. For some, this is a simple bullet point list and some allow and even require pictures and images to be uploaded to external blogs such as Blogger or Tumblr. Some teachers using the Moodle VLE platform use the Mahara plug-in for this. Whatever the tool, many learners can record their reflections on their learning as a 'log' easily and productively using their own mobile devices and sometimes on the bus home or in the library.

Strategy 256 – How does it work? What does it mean?

Consider the two very powerful but deceptively simple questions in the title above. For homework, set one of these questions (depending upon what is appropriate at the time and for the context you are working in) and ask learners to make a presentation to outline and explain an idea or concept from your curriculum area. This presentation could be PowerPoint based, or use Prezi or even your institution's Interactive White Board's own software tools.

Strategy 257 – Fiftysneakers

The online web tool fiftysneakers (fiftysneakers.com) allows teachers to build some stimulating online tests for free. We know of a number of teachers who have used this to good effect and whose students have been very motivated given the rich nature of the design and powerful functionality of the website. Tests made using this website can be set for homework – and used a second time later in the year for revision.

Strategy 258 – Clues

Put online a series of 'clues' to next week's lesson content. Post the clues within your VLE and other online places (blogs, wikis, forums) which learners are directed to as a 'treasure hunt'. Ask learners to follow the clues and to guess the topic of the next lesson – and to say how the content relates and connects to the work already studied.

Strategy 259 – Flip the classroom – record yourself

As another means to develop a 'flipped classroom' (see above) record mini-lectures and then post them on a blog, in YouTube or within your own institution's VLE. Thus, learners access the 'teaching' for homework, listen to/watch the recorded information, make notes and then bring these in. Lessons which run 'face2face' then are flipped – content is 'delivered' for homework and 'teaching time' is used for individual support and differentiated progression.

Strategy 260 – Picture book maker

The website artisancam.org.uk provides a free means for users to create picture books which can then be downloaded and saved. Making a picture book on a curriculum relevant topic (as a way to demonstrate understanding) would be a great homework task – and the final products can be shared amongst peers. You would need to set the theme or topic of the book itself.

Strategy 261 – Traffic lights

This premise can help with AfL strategies both for revision or through the year as a whole. The solution is an eLearning one, but the set-up is both more traditional and very straightforward. At the end of classes or as a starter ask learners, on a regular basis, to reflect upon what they have been learning and what makes sense and what does not. Ask them to 'traffic light' lesson content and curriculum areas on strips of paper – green = all ok; amber = not sure; red = unsure (and needs more help). Use this traffic light coding system to start to see patterns. You can address these patterns through the homework tasks you then subsequently set. Have sections on your VLE where you provide additional tasks, questions, worksheets, information, podcasts, links, etc. for those issues most 'red lighted' and 'amber lighted'. This helps you to be more strategic in your preparation and your learners to be more strategic in homework and revision.

Strategy 262 – You have the whole world in your hands

Rather than a more traditional presentation using a tool such as PowerPoint or even the more non-linear Prezi, ask learners for homework to use *Google Earth* as the basis of their presentation; not to use it to find out information but instead to 'pin' mini presentations and pictures onto locations relevant to the presentation in *Google Earth*. For example, a World War history presentation or a science or literature presentation could pin information to various relevant locations around the virtual globe. In making their presentations to the class in subsequent lessons learners would take the class on a global tour.

Strategy 263 – Clip bank

The 'clip bank' service is provided by UK media channel, Channel 4 (http://clipbank. channel4learning.com/). Institutions will need to sign up for the service but it makes a wide range of video available to teachers to use in both classroom work and homework tasks. Learners could be shown video content in lessons and asked to write or blog reflections on it for homework, for example.

Strategy 264 – Create an ezine

An ezine is an online or digital magazine. Ask learners to run an ezine for you for your subject area. They can post ideas, reviews of useful resources and websites and definitions and quizzes. These ezines can then be distributed to other groups. These can be as simple as a word document which is saved as a PDF document and then uploaded to a VLE or a blog.

Strategy 265 – Polleverywhere I

Polleverywhere (http://www.polleverywhere.com/) is a free to use and simple Web application to build simple 'polls' or voting opportunities over questions you can set. You can set up a series of polls and for homework learners can visit the site through a link you make available to them and vote. The outcome of the polls can be reviewed in the starter of the subsequent lesson.

Strategy 266 – Polleverywhere II

For homework learners could undertake their own primary research using polleverywhere as a tool. They set up a question and distribute the link they receive from the polleverywhere site (http://www.polleverywhere.com/) and use this to generate some simple data that they can then write about.

Strategy 267 – Virtual club

To help stimulate and build interest in your subject area, ask learners for homework (this could be ongoing and longer term) to contribute to the building of a 'virtual club site' representing your subject area and what they have learnt and the value they think your subject has. This club could be housed on a blog or wiki or within the pages of your own VLE. Ask learners to contribute reflections, revision ideas, past homework, photos, etc.

 Strategy 268 – Cause an argument

The Web2.0 tool amap (http://www.amap.org.uk/create/) allows users to generate diagrams rather similar to a mind map but which are based around generating an argument. The user constructs a diagram trying to persuade the viewer of their ideas and opinions. This is very easy to use. For homework learners could access one you have made and then write a response – why they agree/disagree with your argument. Alternatively learners could make ones for themselves and respond to each others' as the starter in the next lesson.

 Strategy 269 – Who wants to be a millionaire?

Ask learners to create their own PowerPoint version of the popular TV quiz show 'Who wants to be a millionaire?'. You could provide the template for them – which slide is which question for which 'amount of money'?. You would need a means to check the accuracy of the content but they could be played by others in class once completed.

Strategy 270 – Zondle

Zondle (https://www.zondle.com/publicPages/welcome.aspx) is a Web2.0 application which lets you create a game for free that can then be viewed and played for free on a smart phone with the required free App. Create revision games and then encourage learners to download the App and use the games as part of their revision homework.

M-it! Strategies 271–300

Why does this matter?

Following on from the previous section (E-it!), in this section we explore ideas that while being 'e-learning' in nature, enable learning to become mobile. Increasingly Mobile or M-learning is referred to as having the possibility of becoming 'U-learning' – of making learning 'ubiquitous' – able to take place any time and any place. Perhaps we are not yet at that point, despite the claims made by some about young people being increasingly 'digital natives' (see Prensky 2001). Nonetheless, mobile learning is a powerful pedagogic tool. In the previous section, E-it!, we have explored the role of technology in creating stimulating and collaborative learning opportunities. Unlike those examples and strategies, these M-it! ideas are not tied down to a desktop PC. With the increasing availability of smartphones, 3G phone signals, mobile internet connections, tablet and other portable handheld devices, and Wi-Fi signals at home, in coffee shops, libraries, schools and colleges learners can engage with learning materials and opportunities in new spaces and places and at new times. While heeding the concerns about the 'digital divide' in the previous section, these final strategies capitalize on this new age of digital moveable technologies.

Strategy 271 – Podcast

Record podcasts using a digital voice recorder or a microphone and a recording software package (such as the freeware Audacity). Try and record short podcasts of between four and eight minutes. These can be uploaded onto your school or college's VLE and downloaded by learners onto phones and other handheld devices where they are playable. Record in MP3 format to ensure compatibility with most devices. These podcasts can aid revision and also can be the 'set-up' for the next lesson and a new topic. Learners could be asked to take notes, write a short summary or answer specific questions based upon what they hear. They do not need to use the audio at home but anywhere they can carry a portable device and wear headphones. Learners can then be questioned about the podcasts at the start of the next lesson.

Strategy 272 – Easy podcasts from a phone

Ask learners to make their own podcasts as homework. Lots of phones and other devices such as portable games machines have the capability to make short recordings for example, or they could be issued with digital voice recorders. Webcams also come with integrated mics, although this would make them less mobile. Learners can make revision recordings for each other which can then be consumed by others.

Strategy 273 – Podcast your feedback

Provide feedback to learners in an audio form based upon previous work and assessments. Learners can be provided with a personalized audio recording that you have made with specific advice for them to consider when completing a similar piece of work in the future – say an essay or a test paper or part of an assignment. Learners can download the podcast and carry it around with them on phones, etc., ready to be used when they approach the next piece of work. The homework from this would be for learners to undertake formal self-evaluation, documenting what they have understood from your feedback. Finally, encourage learners to record their self-evaluation as a podcast back to you!

Strategy 274 – Using QR codes

QR stands for quick response. These codes are essentially barcodes which many companies make use of in printed materials to direct readers to their websites or online stores. QR codes (see Figure 7.1) can be made extremely easily by anyone with an internet connection. Websites such as Kaywa (http://qrcode.kaywa.com/) allow you to insert a URL internet address and within seconds you can create a unique coded picture which contains within it the digital information needed to link to that particular webaddress. This means that on handouts you can insert your own tailor-made QR codes alongside tasks and activities. Smartphones such as the iPhone and Android can download free apps which allow the user of the phone to 'read' the QR code using the built-in camera function. On opening the app

Figure 7.1 Example of a QR Code

and 'reading' the coded image the smartphone instantly takes the user to the very webaddress coded into the digital information. This means learners can work on a worksheet and, using mobile devices, have the ability to go straight to key websites to help them complete the tasks. This means they can complete the work anywhere – not just at a desktop PC.

Strategy 275 – Tweet tweet

Twitter – the micro-blogging service – can be used by teachers to set homework tasks. It can also be used for announcements and reminders. If using Twitter, teachers are reminded of the need for digital safety and are asked to check within their institution for the digital safety regulations which govern and safeguard their online practice and that of their learners. As an example of a homework Tweet (remembering that you only have 140 characters to use including spaces and punctuation), learners could be asked to:

Create a 5 min Prezi presentation http://prezi.com/ demonstrating what you have learnt from our topic in class to date; to present to everyone at start next lesson (137 characters in all).

In addition to using Twitter for homework announcements and using Yammer for debates and discussions, Twitter can also be used as a means to easily distribute key links and reading to learners.

 ## Strategy 276 – Make a movie 1

Using free movie maker software which comes bundled in with most laptops and desktops it is relatively simple to make short films. Teachers could make films introducing learners to key topics or new subjects using images, captions and audio. These films can be distributed to learners (by email, on a VLE or learners could download them); the movies can then form the basis of the introduction to the next topic. Quiz learners on these movies in the next session (as a starter activity) or even ask them to make their own movies in response.

 ## Strategy 277 – Using folksonomies

'Folksonomies' is the term given to the practice where we see user-generated attempts to clarify and categorize. Folksonomies capture how ordinary people, collaboratively, seek to define and give meaning to internet and web-based objects (pages, images, pictures, videos, etc.) by organizing them to make sense of them. Set tasks where learners need to visit webpages or other online content such as images and pictures or podcasts and start to rank, code and classify them for each other. Ask learners to bring in these codes and categories and support each other in class in using and understanding a range of sources which they can then use in their own assignments and class work.

Strategy 278 – 'Get your phones out please'

Ask learners to use cameras in phones to capture key images which summarize or link to topics under discussion in class. Rather than start the lesson with the reminder 'put your phones away, please' you could turn this on its head. Ask them to 'get your phones out, please' and share the images they have taken to get them all talking at the start of a lesson.

> **BEST PRACTICE – BYOD**
>
> This is a controversial point and for many teachers will not be possible given institutional rules about learners having technological devices on them. You might also be cautious of this if you are aware of a digital divide amongst the learners you teach. These warnings in place, BYOD stands for 'bring your own device' and is but one element in what we are increasingly calling a 'flipped classroom'. In this classroom, you allow learners to bring and use whatever appropriate device they feel comfortable working on – hence the suggestion in Strategy 278 to 'get your phones out'. This means that homework is completed digitally and mobile devices are brought in so that the work can then be shared with the teacher and other learners. This might make it easier for some to complete tasks and also encourages a degree of independence and choice in working and learning practices.

Strategy 279 – Get blogging

Ask learners to keep a blog or an online diary of their thoughts and opinions about a topic linked to their studies. Alternatively, if possible and appropriate, the blogs themselves could contribute to assessed work – they could showcase their art work, writing, etc. You would need to decide how visible they were to public eyes and what they did and did not say about themselves. You would also need to manage the process so that private and personal work was not open for others to copy. Most smartphones come with apps which would allow learners to access their blog on the move.

Strategy 280 – Open surgery

Agree a time once a week where you will be logged onto a forum or wiki inside your school or college's VLE or using Twitter or Yammer. In 'real time' (what we can synchronously) learners know you are receiving messages and they can seek you out and ask for help and clarity over homework tasks you have set. For example, ask them to use a piece of social media (blog, Twitter, Yammer, etc.) to make a diary of their learning – the 'key messages' from each lesson for a set period of time. You can then arrange to support this work by offering guidance in the above online means.

Strategy 281 – Micro-blog surgery support

This strategy works not in real time but is what we call asynchronous. Set up a Twitter or Yammer account and use this to provide support to learners as they need it. They can post comments and questions seeking guidance and support and you are free to respond as and when you can. After receiving support on homework the follow-up homework would be for the learners to document/record what they have learnt from the feedback. They could use a blog of a piece of micro-blogging such as Twitter or Yammer to do this.

Strategy 282 – Using SMS

You would need clear guidelines and institutional permission for this suggestion. You may also need parental permission. Use text messaging (called SMS) to send homework updates and reminders to learners. Following on from this, SMS or text messages could be used as a form of support and guidance. You could send out homework reminders and organize drop-in support sessions and peer-led working groups.

 ## Strategy 283 – Collaborative filtering

The process of 'collaborative filtering' means to work as part of a group on a document/project/text where everyone can edit everyone else's work. A simple way to do this is through GoogleDocs. All members of the group are given a password access to the same document which can be updated and edited by multiple users (even at the same time). This is an excellent opportunity to encourage learners to work cooperatively and also asynchronously. As with many of these strategies, with recent developments in mobile phones, mobile computing and mobile devices, this type of collaborative work can take place anywhere and on the move. This makes the act of collaboration between learners different from previously where learners were fixed to the same location at the same time or tied to a desktop PC in order to get online.

Strategy 284 – Social bookmarking

Social bookmarking (similarly to the construction of 'folksonomies' – see Strategy 277) refers to the act of multiple users 'tagging' or bookmarking sites and links of interest with the view of sharing these with others. An easy to use way of doing this is through websites such as delicious (http://www.delicious.com/) although there are many such services available. Learners can create lists of bookmarks for homework and can then share them with their peers. Subsequently, when completing other homework tasks they can draw upon the social bookmarking lists when doing research.

Strategy 285 – Making posters with Glogster.Com

Glogster.com allows you to mix text, images and graphics together to make an 'interactive' poster. These can then be shared between users. This would be an excellent homework with learners making their own posters and then showing them as a starter for the next class. Alternatively they could be created at another time and homework could be to use each others' posters to answer key questions on a given topic.

Strategy 286 – Diigo chain

Diigo stands for 'Digest of internet information, groups and other stuff' and is one of the most recent social bookmarking spaces. When you highlight a word on any page on the net a dropdown menu appears that allows you to search for highlighted words on the web, bookmarking systems, blogs, etc. It offers a visually stunning way for learners to follow research trajectories. Set up a group for your class asking them to research a particular topic. Each learner must put three relevant links up on Diigo. This homework allows you to see instantly how students are engaging with their subject and it provides a fabulous resource for all learners in that group.

Strategy 287 – Yammer debate

Yammer is a collaborative 'micro-blogging' service which shares some similarity with Twitter. Yammer is more secure, only allowing collaborators with the same institutional email address to share and communicate. We think Yammer is a great tool to encourage short debate and interaction between learners. Yammer can be accessed from any smartphone with an internet connection and posts are short enough not to take too much time. It is not dissimilar to the texting that younger learners do incredibly speedily. Set debates and discussions on Yammer around central questions. Stretch learners with thought-provoking, open-ended questions. One of the consequences of using services such as this is that you have a readily available record of who contributed what and how frequently, which would come in handy for assessment purposes.

Strategy 288 – Monitoring reading

If you are using Twitter or Yammer to provide reading to your learners you might like to find a way to start to measure the impact of this. One way of doing this is to set the

Figure 7.2   Screen shot of bit.ly

reading and links as homework and then link this to the starter of the next lesson – maybe a quiz or ask learners to make presentations of what they have read. You could 'jigsaw' this and provide some links for some learners and different ones for others. If you do 'jigsaw' the homework then this means that learners will need to provide feedback to each other at some point so that the whole 'picture' is completed. If you use a URL shortening service (such as bit.ly – http://bit.ly/: see Figure 7.2) you can not only reduce space by shortening the URL down (for fitting on Twitter, for example) but you also get to produce a unique code which will allow you to track how many links to your desired site go through the code you have distributed.

This should help you to see how quickly learners respond to your messages and Tweets and over what period of time.

Strategy 289 – Make a Wordle

Wordle (http://www.wordle.net/) is a simple means to create images and pictures based upon 'tag cloud' aesthetics (see Figure 7.3).

Wordles allow the user to cut and paste text into a Java-based website which at a click of a button creates a tag cloud design. The user can experiment with the font, colour and layout and can even isolate some words. Wordle also has the capacity to allow the user to begin to categorize words and their frequency in the text used to create the design in the first place. For homework learners can be asked to make Wordles rather than create posters or revision notes which they can then share with others.

Figure 7.3   Example of a Wordle

Strategy 290 – Make a movie 2

Most mobile phones (and other handheld devices) have the ability to record short video footage. Learners could be asked to make a movie on a topic and upload them to a space on the VLE ready to be shared amongst the class. Alternatively, if budgets permit, simple video recorders (such as the FlipCam) can be purchased by teams and loaned out.

Strategy 291 – SMS quizzes

A series of quiz questions are texted to learners straight onto their mobile phones. This can be done all in one go or over a longer duration. The quizzes can be answered and texted back to you.

Strategy 292 – SMS 'walk around'

This approach to using SMS or text messages for quizzes was adopted with very positive outcomes in the LSN Mobile Learning in Practice project (Savill-Smith et al. 2006). Learners are given access to flyers, handouts or posters around their school and college environment with a series of quiz questions. They can text in their answer to the phone number advertised and answers can be recorded and marked either by yourself or whoever receives the SMS.

Strategy 293 – Create an on-the-go digital mind map

Many handheld devices have the ability for learners to make sketches and draw diagrams – sometimes with a touch screen and sometimes by using a stylus. Any mobile screen that allows for sketching and drawing can therefore be used to make mind maps and other such mapping diagrams. Mobile devices free up the user to be able to create these on the move – on the bus, in the library – wherever the inspiration comes. Such maps once created could be uploaded or emailed to teachers for assessment and also shared collaboratively amongst peers. Many smartphones come with this technology available through apps.

Strategy 294 – Make a flip-book

Many handheld devices with upgradeable and downloadable wigits, plug-ins and apps have the ability to make old fashioned 'flip-books' – each screen, replicating a flick or turn of the page, leads to a new drawing which as the pages/screen progress through create a simple animation, such as a stick-person walking. This is a simple way to create a little animated story which for homework could be used to illustrate a story/process/case study/example from a lesson.

Strategy 295 – Google jockeying

This process is really worth considering and adapting if you are requiring learners to work collaboratively on a joint project outside of the class. A 'Google Jockey' is a peer who takes the role to use the internet to surf for ideas, links, terms, information, etc. linked to the work someone else is presenting and explaining to a group. This 'jockeying' is done in real time. By the end of the presentation the group have a wide range of sources to then explore further, based upon the original presentation from their peers. This is now easy to set up in the class if learners are using handheld devices. For homework or learning outside of the class you could set up groups who are required to teach something to each other. At the same time peers can be ascribed the role of the 'Google jockey' to add further depth to this collaboration.

Strategy 296 – Utilizing the backchannel

The term 'backchannel' in this context refers to the use of social media (such as Twitter) by audiences to commentate on life real-life events they are watching, while they are watching them. A further discussion of this phenomena can be found in the 2010 book *The Backchannel: How Audiences are Using Twitter and Social Media and Changing Presentations Forever* by Cliff Atkinson. Teachers could deploy this in their classes – having a 'live' Twitter stream posted up in the class for learners to commentate upon the lesson. Alternatively, learners could be taken to conferences or gallery/museum trips outside of the classroom and be asked to use Twitter and other such social media to record notes and thoughts accessible to all members of the group.

Strategy 297 – Google moderator

'Google moderator' is a free service, part of the Google group of services, that lets pre-defined groups and audiences vote on questions set in advance. The service then collates the outcomes of the voting and makes this available to all those who took part. This could be very useful as a means to moderate discussions between learners. Homework could be to contribute a given number of times to a discussion or debate and then to complete the task by voting on the ideas of others. This can then be discussed further the very next lesson.

Strategy 298 – Moving pictures

Developing on from some of the ideas in Strategy 213, ask learners to use readily available mobile technology (camera phones, etc.) to create a photo-story or photo-montage on a particular topic. Get learners to then present their creation to the group or write something about it, explaining and justifying how the choice of images link to the topic or theme they have been asked to think about. These presentations could be used as starter activities for the start of subsequent lessons.

Strategy 299 – Mobile mood board

Taking the ideas in Strategy 298 (and 293) slightly further, learners could be asked to create a 'mood board' – a pictorial representation of how they feel about a given topic/issue. This could use mobile technology to capture the images or even to present the mood board in a digital way as a poster (see Strategy 293 for ideas on this).

Strategy 300 – The field trip: combine blogging and note taking with collaboration

The ideas in this M-it! section are powerful (and often relatively simple) ways to harness mobile/portable technology and devices and use them to transfer ideas, share links and information and to record thoughts. Many of them have at their heart a notion of learning as collaboration. Although straightforward, they work best when combined together, for example, with learners making podcasts and using blogs to record thoughts or presenting blogs to each other while some peers 'Google jockey' and others still use social media backchannels. Combining these different ways to collaborate together adds a distinctive richness to learning outside the classroom. Nowhere is this more effective than in the field trip, especially if it is an educational visit to a gallery or museum. Sites already exist for learners who make visits to galleries (see myartspace – http://www.myartspace.com/) to create blogs where they document the experiences and share these.

Part 3

What next? And your homework is...

8   Looking back and looking forwards

Chapter objectives

In this chapter we will:

- understand the importance of critical reflection in HfL;
- explore the role that learner voice can play in developing your HfL strategies;
- consider the ways in which action research can enhance your own professional practice and the practice within your institution;
- discuss and reflect upon the variety of ways you can create your own homework strategies.

Introduction – taking time to reflect

The view that outstanding teachers are constantly engaged with the self-assessment and evaluation of their own practice as a key aspect of their ongoing professionalism is an ideal and one that many teachers rightly aspire to. And yet, as we have mentioned earlier, the multiple demands placed on many teachers within and beyond the confines of their classroom make this process at best challenging, and at worst nigh on impossible. But if HfL is to become embedded within your professional teaching and learning repertoire we argue that this process of critical reflection is essential and that homework provides an invaluable opportunity to review and evaluate the efficacy of the teaching and learning strategies you deploy and facilitate. As we move into this final chapter we offer an opportunity to pause for thought and consider your own critical reflective practice and how you can develop your own emerging HfL philosophy.

What do we mean by 'reflection'?

It has long been recognized that for effective teaching to take place, teachers need to unite both theory and practice – they are two sides of the same coin and underpin HfL. Practice uninformed by theory is never going to be critical and will be blinkered – it will always be kept in the dark. Whereas theory uninformed by practice will be pointless and merely abstract. Uniting theory and practice is essential for sound reflective thinking – being able to see the connections between what you do, how you feel about it, how you evaluate it and what research and theory also tells you. The unification of theory and practice is referred to as 'praxis': attempts to link them result in a far greater outcome than simply having theory and practice separate from each other. In this chapter we provide a variety of ways for you to engage in this process in relation to your own homework strategies.

?

FREQUENTLY ASKED QUESTIONS – WHAT IS REFLECTION?

Much of the existing teacher education literature draws upon the idea of reflection. The notion of reflection is seen in a variety of ways:

1. Reflection is a means to improve one's own practice through criticism and evaluation.
2. It is a means through which practitioners can 'de-bunk' their prior assumptions, leading to a greater insight.
3. Being reflective is seen as a major part of the critical and 'distanced' role to be adopted by all professionals, teachers included.
4. Reflectivity is seen as a means through which to better construct one's own professional identity and to better know one's professional self.
5. Reflection is a means towards 'praxis': it can allow professionals the space to make connections between their practice and the wider theoretical concerns.

Reflection is the act of 'meaning-making' – putting order and sense onto the world around you. As a professional teacher it involves thinking about the role you are occupying, your own actions and practice within this role, and how and why things happen as they do. It allows you to think about why some things do not happen. In relation to HfL, reflection is seen as a vehicle through which to explore practice that has not as yet happened. It is a form of introspection with the goal of self-improvement.

The term 'reflective practitioner' coined by Schön (1983) makes use of two different notions of reflection and reflective practice:

1. reflection in action;
2. reflection on action.

While reflection in action is 'thinking on our feet', making choices as we do them 'in the moment', reflection on action occurs after the event. Reflection on action takes the memory of the experience or the event and allows us the time and space to think about it with the kind of hindsight that enables the drawing together of other linked experiences. Through reflection on action, after the action itself, we can make connections, apply theory and seek the advice and support of mentors, peers and other colleagues. Experienced practitioners are able to draw upon the sum total of their thoughts, reflections and engagement with theory in the moment, the more used they become to reflection after the moment. Through the combination of both types of reflection you can increase your 'stock' and efficacy of HfL strategies and resources at any given moment. The following twenty questions are designed to help you in this reflective process.

20 questions for reflection on HfL

1. What are your own strengths and weaknesses in terms of the homework activities you set?
2. What are the strengths and weaknesses of the homework policy in the institution in which you are employed?
3. When was the last time you consulted your own learners about the types of homework they enjoy, value and learn best from?
4. What opportunities exist outside your teaching institution to provide innovative homework activities?
5. Who, in your own institution of learning, are the leading homework practioners and have you sought their advice in terms of your own professional practice?
6. What professional development would be most appropriate for you to increase the efficacy of your homework strategies?
7. What homework strategies have you tended to adopt the most and the least and are you aware why this is the case?
8. How many of the strategies in this book have you tried and are you logging how successful they are?
9. What might you learn from other colleagues and how can you accommodate their practice into your own?
10. In what ways do your homework strategies reflect ideas associated with AfL?
11. How do you know if an idea for homework practice is worth trying?
12. Against what measurements do you assess the success of your homework strategies?
13. How can you tell what the impact and effects of your practice are?
14. In what ways do you monitor formatively, summatively and ipsatively the homework performance of your learners?
15. In what ways do you reflect on this performance when redesigning or updating your schemes of work?
16. How do you and your institution manage educational visits? What role does homework play in the facilitation of visits?
17. To what extent do you expect all your learners to complete homework for you and in what ways do you communicate those expectations?
18. Are you aware of the homework strategies deployed in both vocational and academic subjects within the institution you work in? To what extent do colleagues share practice from both arenas of learning?
19. To what extent can your homework activities successfully fulfil Kolb's learning cycle objectives?
20. Do you consult the learning support staff when creating your homework activities and the resources that accompany them? To what extent do you offer the

opportunity for them to feed back to you their thoughts on how tasks could be better designed/facilitated?

LINKING THEORY WITH PRACTICE

A popular and well-regarded model of the role of reflection and experience in learning is provided by David Kolb (Kolb and Fry 1975). Kolb's learning cycle can be applied to all learners and their teachers when considering the effectiveness of homework strategies. For Kolb, there are four processes to undertake when engaging in critical reflection – and each process follows the next, in sequence, as a cycle:

1. Concrete Experience
2. Reflective Observation
3. Abstract Conceptualization
4. Active Experimentation

Put simply, you have an experience – you 'do something' within your own practice (Concrete Experience). You then make a judgment on this initial experience; you analyse it and reflect upon it building meaning as you do so (Reflective Observation). In this stage you start to ask yourself questions about the meaning and significance of the experience. When thinking about how we might improve on the practice next time (Abstract Conceptualization) we think into the future using our experience as a template to action plan and imagine future practice as yet conducted. Finally, we try out the new practice (Active Experimentation), and then engage in the cycle all over again. For learners successful homework strategies provide an invaluable opportunity to engage in these processes of reflection. Teachers can also benefit from this model when reflecting on the success of their strategies and how they can be improved in future.

LINKING THEORY WITH PRACTICE

In Part 1 of the book we learnt that relatively little research has been done on the effects of homework on the post-16 environment and how little we know of its impact on vocational subjects. We also know that teacher expectation plays a vital role in the completion rates of all tasks including those set in homework. To what extent have you reflected on differences in the expectations of teachers in terms of the tasks given to 'academic' and 'vocational' learners? If you teach both sorts of pupil or student, to what extent do you differentiate between these two group? To what extent do you believe that the latter group may generally be given less exciting or challenging homework activities? Do you believe there is scope to re-think the homework tasks we give to vocational learners and those in the post-16 learning environment?

Consulting and listening to learners' views on homework

Although there has been considerable research carried out on the relationship between homework and its effects on educational achievement we know relatively little about younger learners' perceptions of homework (see Hallam 2005; Kohn 2006; Warton 2001), how they perceive teacher and parental viewpoints and how these views might change over time. Student (or 'pupil') voice has been the subject of considerable academic debate and is now grabbing the attention of policy makers, examination boards, government ministers and journalists. The most significant driving force for this movement internationally is the United Nations Convention on the Rights of the Child (UNCRC) acknowledging the rights of all children to be consulted on all aspects of their education, including the homework strategies they engage with. While many schools and colleges are still reluctant to 'listen' to the voices of those that make up its majority there are many benefits to be gained. Halsey et al. (2006) argue that these include:

- improvements in learner services (e.g. improvements in canteen and toilet facilities);
- improvements in decision making (e.g. giving learners more of a say in the financial decisions taken by schools/colleges);
- greater democracy for learners (e.g. allowing learners a say in which teachers are employed; how long lessons run for; influencing subjects offered and the homework policies inititated);
- fulfilling legal requirements within schools/colleges (e.g. in terms of 'citizenship' and the UNCRC);
- enhancing learners' skills (e.g. allowing learners to run meetings with staff; including learners on interview panels);
- empowering learner self-esteem (e.g. increasing self-confidence and status when learners are consulted by their peers and teachers).

However in many schools and colleges where learner voice operates, only a minority of learners has an opportunity to voice their opinions. Learning institutions are, in most cases, hierarchical structures (e.g. power rests with the board of governors and head and senior management of the institution). They are also hierarchical in terms of learners, i.e. older learners tend to have greater 'voice' and status within most schools. Quite often formal and informal segregation by age, class, gender, ethnicity and ability restricts the 'voices' of many learners in institutions where learner voice operates. As advocates of learner voice we would therefore strongly recommend that all learners:

- are consulted on the types of homework strategies they value, and the means in which these activities are assessed;
- are given sufficient opportunity during the course of their studies to decide the types of activities they can produce in response to the specific assessment criteria on their courses;
- are provided with opportunities to engage in peer marking activities associated with the homework strategies they are given;

- are given the opportunity to become co-researchers with other teachers on the action research projects designed to examine the role that homework can play in school/college life and the life of the learner.

Echoing the thoughts of Warton (2001) homework strategies are unlikely to successfully contribute to the development of generic skills such as time management and learner autonomy unless they are valued by learners themselves. Consulting them and actively putting into practice their thoughts on the matter would seem a valuable way forward for all institutions of learning and the professionals that work within them.

Action research on homework strategies in your own institution

While research has established homework as a viable and successful means to raise achievement (when initiated and facilitated under the right conditions) there is little within the literature to provide recommendations to practitioners as to how best to do this. Action research is practitioner-based research where the researcher adopts transformative practices often based on reflection and experimentation with a view to developing aspects of their practice (and in some cases the practices in their institution) further. In recent years action research for educational practitioners has risen to the fore as a means through which teachers can investigate and explore their own practice (see Baumfield et al. 2008). This development is often linked in the literature to the emphasis within the professional field on reflective practice and to the idea that schools and colleges are places or communities of learning at every level and that therefore, teachers within the same learning institutions are members of a 'community of practice' (Wenger 1998). The role that homework can play in raising achievement, motivation and enjoyment is a topic ideal for action research although perhaps surprisingly one that is under researched in institutions of learning.

According to McNiff and Whitehead (2006) and Koshy (2005) action research is a distinctive approach to practitioners' research. Since it is 'action' and 'research' at the same time, this sort of research is often carried out by practitioners into their own practice. Thus, the classroom teacher, usually through experimentation and reflection, is both a researcher and a practitioner at the same time. In occupying both roles in this way, the outcome of action research is practical knowledge, which can then lead to further change in one's own practice. The process of action research, as with any research processes, involves the identification of a research problem or question – something the practitioner has noticed that they think warrants further consideration and investigation, for example, what role does the implementation of homework play in more successful exam based subjects in your own institution? The practitioner identifies the procedures for capturing data and documenting their analysis of this data and their reflections on the process. This commitment to practitioner research is a very powerful tool for encouraging teacher autonomy and continuing reflective practice as well as offering something of tremendous value to colleagues within and outside your institution. This is an excellent means through which to continue your professional development which is why we offer the twenty questions on pages 163 for you to reflect on in terms of your own professional development and also as a means to a possible action research project in your own institution.

Generating your own homework strategies

Benjamin Bloom (1956) and his classic 'taxonomy' of learning offers teachers a framework for creating and evaluating different types of homework. Originally designed as a classification of goals within any education system his taxonomy focused around three domains: the cognitive (including knowledge, intellectual abilities and skills); the affective (including interests, attitudes, emotions and values) and the psycho-motor (ranging from simple reflex movements to more advanced articulation and kinaesthetic activities, e.g. dancing/sport, etc). Drawing on the work of Bloom (1956), Anderson and Krathwohl (2001) have created a classification of educational objectives focused around thinking skills. Table 8.1 below shows these skills. Experiment by using this table when creating and planning homework strategies incorporating each of the thinking skills into your range of homework activities.

The activity in Table 8.2 draws together Gardner's work on multiple intelligences (1993) (see Chapter 1) and the work of Anderson and Krathwohl (2001). Use this template to generate as many differentiated homework strategies as possible.

And finally...

We hope you have enjoyed this book and the ideas and strategies that we have presented and discussed. We certainly do not make any claims that by 'magicking' up a range of

Table 8.1 Thinking skills homework activity matrix

Thinking skills	Examples of instruction words for your homework activities	Homework activity
Remembering	who? when? what? recall; list; define; name; describe	
Understanding	why? summarize; contrast; interpret; discuss; translate	
Applying	solve; classify; discover; predict; apply; demonstrate	
Analysing	compare and contrast; connect; analyse; order; explain; separate	
Evaluating	rank; summarize; evaluate; conclude; assess; decide	
Creating	compose; design; integrate; modify; combine	

Table 8.2 Homework activity matrix comparing learning skills and learning styles

	Linguistic	Logical-mathematical	Spatial	Bodily-Kinaesthetic	Musical	Interpersonal	Intrapersonal
Remembering	match the…						
Understanding		Identify trends in…					
Applying			Draw a diagram that…				Write a short story about…
Analysing							
Evaluating					Compose a song with lyrics that…		
Creating						Take part in a mini-election in which your party must…	

homework strategies your learners will perform wonders in their exams, projects, exhibitions and so on. But we do promise that their learning experience will be enhanced, your teaching will be enriched and in years to come your pupils/students will remember you and your subject with warmth, enthusiasm and gratitude. If the evidence for and against homework is confusing, don't wait for the 'experts' to decide for you. The homework debate has been around for much of the twentieth century and continues well into the twenty-first with little sign of abating. As a professional educator one of your jobs is to continue to be informed and reflect on the latest research in hand, critically engaging with the ideas within your own learning communities using your own professional judgement and first hand experience to develop your own professional practice. In this final chapter we hope we have given you some tools in which to turn those professional reflections into research informed practice. Your homework starts here – good luck!

> **QUESTIONS FOR PROFESSIONAL DEVELOPMENT**
>
> 1. How many of the 20 questions for reflection were you able to successfully answer? What insights do the answers to these questions have on your own professional practice? In what ways could you initiate change for the better that will affect positively the educational outcomes of your learners?
> 2. In what ways can you build in the voice of your learners into the homework strategies you engage in? Could you, for example, develop a questionnaire at the start of the academic year that provides you with useful information regarding what works best for them as an assessment strategy?
> 3. In what ways can you revisit your own strategies for engaging learners with off-site visits?
> 4. Do you keep any sort of professional reflective journal? If the answer is 'yes' then in what ways can you use this to note down and reflect upon successful and less successful homework strategies and how you can build more successful practice in your professional repertoire in future?

Bibliography

Anderson, L.W. and Krathwohl D. (eds) (2001) *A Taxonomy for Learning, Teaching and Assessing: A Revision of Bloom's Taxonomy of Educational Objectives*. New York: Longman.

Assessment Reform Group (2002) *Testing, Motivation and Learning*. Cambridge: University of Cambridge.

Atkinson, C. (2010) *The Backchannel: How Audiences are Using Twitter and Social Media and Changing Presentations Forever*. Berkeley, CA: New Riders.

Baumfield, V., Hall, E. and Wall, K. (2008) *Action Research in the Classroom*. London: Sage.

Black, P. and Wiliam, D. (1998) *Inside the Black Box: Raising Standards Through Classroom Assessment*. London: Kings College.

Bloom, B. (1956) *Taxonomy of Educational Objectives. Handbook 1: Cognitive Domain*. New York: David McKay.

Bourdieu, P. (1977) *Outline of a Theory of Practice*. Cambridge: Cambridge University Press.

Bourdieu, P. (1990) Structures, habitus, practices. In P. Bourdieu, *The Logic of Practice* (pp. 52–79). Stanford, CA: Stanford University Press.

Brookfield, S. (1995) *Becoming a Critically Reflective Teacher*. San Francisco, CA: Jossey-Bass.

Cooper, H. (1989) *Homework*. New York: Longman.

Cross, J. (2006) *Informal Learning: Rediscovering the Natural Pathways that Inspire Innovation and Performance*. London: John Wiley and Sons.

Czerniawski, G. (2011) *Emerging Teachers and Globalisation*. London: Routledge.

de Bono, E. (2009) *Six Thinking Hats*. London: Penguin.

Dennison, B. and Kirk, R. (1990) *Do Review Learn Apply: A Simple Guide to Experiential Learning*. Oxford: Blackwell.

Dobbs, K. (2000) Simple moments of learning. *Training*, 35(1): 52–8.

Falk, J.H., Dierking, L.D. and Foutz, S. (2007) *Learning from Museums: Visitor Experiences and the Making of Meaning*. Lanham: AltaMira Press.

Fröbel, F. (1900) *The Student's Froebel: Adapted from 'Die Erziehung der Menschheit' of F. Froebel*, by W. Herford (2 vols). London: Isbister.

Gardner, H. (1993) *Frames of Mind: The Theory of Multiple Intelligences*. New York: Basic Books.

Glick, M. (2006) *The Instructional Leader and the Brain: Using Neuroscience to Inform Practice*. London: Corwin.

Goleman, D. (1995) *Emotional Intelligence*. New York: Bantham.

Gonzalez, C. (2004) *The Role of Blended Learning in the World of Technology*. http://www.unt.edu/benchmarks/archives/2004/september04/eis.htm (accessed 15 October 2012).

Hallam, S. (2004) *Homework: The Evidence*. London: Styles Publications.

Hallam, S. (2005) Making decisions about homework: what the evidence tells us. *NSIN Research Matters*, 25: 1–8.

Halsey, K., Gulliver, C., Johnson, A., Martin, K. and Kinder, K. (2006) *Evaluation of Behaviour and Education Support Teams*. London: DfES.

Hancock, J. (2001) *Homework: A Literature Review*. Occasional Paper published by the College of Education and Human Development. University of Maine, Shibles Hall.

Hase, S. and Kenyon, C. (2007) Heutagogy: a child of complexity theory. *Complicity: An International Journal of Complexity and Education*, 4(1): 111–18.

Henderson, J.M. (2006) Power Relations within the homework process. Unpublished PhD thesis, University of Stirling.

Howard-Jones, P. (2002) *Neuroscience and Education: Issues and Opportunities*. London: Teaching and Learning Research Programme.

James, M. and Pollard, A. (2006) *Improving Teaching and Learning in Schools*. London: TLRP.

Kidd, W. and Czerniawski, G. (2010) *Successful Teaching 14–19: Theory, Practice and Reflection*. London: Sage.

Kidd, W. and Czerniawski, G. (2011) *Teaching Teenagers: A Toolbox for Engaging and Motivating Learners*. London: Sage.

Knowles, M.S. (1980) *The Modern Practice of Adult Education: Andragogy Versus Pedagogy*. Cambridge: Prentice Hall.

Kohn, A. (2006) *The Homework Myth: Why our Kids Get Too Much of a Bad Thing*. Cambridge: De Capo Press.

Kolb, D.A. and Fry, R. (1975) Toward an applied theory of experiential learning. In C. Cooper (ed.) *Theories of Group Process*. London: John Wiley.

Koshy, V. (2005) *Action Research for Improving Practice: A Practical Guide*. London: Sage.

Lave, J. and Wenger, E. (1991) *Situated Learning: Legitimate Peripheral Participation*. Cambridge: Cambridge University Press.

Le Doux, J.E. (2002) *Synaptic Self: How Our Brains Become Who We Are*. London: Penguin Putnam.

Leach, J. and Moon, B. (2008) *The Power of Pedagogy*. London: Sage.

Macbeath, J. and Turner, M. (1990) *Learning out of School: Homework, Policy and Practice*. A Research Study commissioned by the Scottish Education Department. Glasgow: Jordan Hill College.

McGregor, D. (2007) *Developing Thinking, Developing Learning: A Guide to Thinking Skills in Education*. Maidenhead: Open University Press.

McNeil, F. (1999) *SIN Research Matters: Brain Research and Learning – An Introduction*. No. 10. London: School Improvement Network.

McNiff, J. and Whitehead, J. (2006) *All You Need to Know about Action Research*. London: Sage.

Montessori, M. (1909) *The Montessori Method: Scientific Pedagogy as Applied to Child Education in 'the Children's Houses'*. New York: Frederic A. Stokes Company.

Muis, D. and Reynolds, D. (2011) *Effective Teaching: Evidence and Practice*. London: Sage.

Patell, E., Cooper, H. and Robinson, J.C. (2009) Parental involvement in homework – a research synthesis. *Review of Educational Research*, 78(4): 1039–101.

Powlov, I.P. (1927) *Conditional Reflexes*. London: Routledge and Kegan Paul.

Prensky, M. (2010) *Teaching Digital Natives: Partnering for Real Learning*. San Diego, CA: Corwin.

Prensky, M. (2001) 'Digital natives, digital immigrants Part 1'. *On The Horizon – The Strategic Planning Resource for Educational Professionals*, 9(5): 51–64.

Rogers, C. (1969) *Freedom to Learn*. New York: Macmillan/Merrill.

Savill-Smith, C., Attewell, J. and Stead, G. (2006) *Mobile Learning in Practice: Piloting a Mobile Learning Teachers' Toolkit in Further Education Colleges*. London: LSN.

Schön, D.A. (1983) *The Reflective Practitioner: How Practitioners think in Action*. London: Temple Smith.

Selwyn, N. (2009) The digital native – myth and reality. *Aslib Proceedings: New Information Perspectives*, 61(4): 364–79.

Siemens, G. (2004) *Connectivism: A Learning Theory for the Digital Age*. http://www.elearnspace.org/Articles/connectivism.htm (accessed 15 March 2013).

Skinner, B.F. (1957) *Verbal Behavior*. Englewood Cliffs, NJ: Prentice Hall.

Soloman, Y., Warin, J. and Lewis, C. (2002) Helping with homework? Homework as a site of tension for parents and teenagers. *British Educational Research Journal*, 28(4): 124–9.

Thorndyke, E.L. (1911) *Animal Intelligence*. London: Macmillan.

Vygotsky, L.S. (1978) *Mind and Society: The Development of Higher Psychological Processes*. Cambridge, MA: Harvard University Press.

Walker, J.M.T., Hoover-Dempsey, K.V., Whetsel, D.R. and Green, C.L. (2004) *Parental Involvement with Homework*. Harvard: Harvard Family Research Project.

Warton, P.M. (2001) The forgotten voices of homework: views of students. *Educational Psychologist*, 36(3): 155—65.

Watson, J.B. (1913) Psychology as the behaviorist views it. *Psychological Review*, 20: 158–77.

Wenger, R. (1998) *Communities of Practice: Learning, Meaning and Identity*. Cambridge: Cambridge University Press.

Index